"With dedication and devotion to her profession and her readers, Stefanie Stolinsky has skillfully created a meaningful approach to a healing journey of self-help for those whose lives have been marred by traumas of abuse. Founded on sound theoretical knowledge and clinical experience, it is beautifully lucid and illuminating."

—Donna Young Sexsmith, Ph.D., in private practice, Los Angeles, California.

Act It Out

25 Expressive Ways to Heal from Childhood Abuse

Stefanie Auerbach Stolinsky, Ph.D.

New Harbinger Publications, Inc.

Publisher's Note

This publication is designed to provide accurate and authoritative information in regard to the subject matter covered. It is sold with the understanding that the publisher is not engaged in rendering psychological, financial, legal, or other professional services. If expert assistance or counseling is needed, the services of a competent professional should be sought.

All case histories are a compelation of many different stories in order to maintain confidentiality.

Distributed in the U.S.A. by Publishers Group West; in Canada by Raincoast Books; in Great Britain by Airlift Book Company, Ltd.; in South Africa by Real Books, Ltd.; in Australia by Boobook; and in New Zealand by Tandem Press.

New Harbinger Publications, Inc.
5674 Shattuck Avenue
Oakland, CA 94609

Cover design by Blue Designs
Edited by Carole Honeychurch
Text design by Tracy Marie Carlson

ISBN 1-57224-290-6 Paperback

Printed in the United States of America

New Harbinger Publications' Web site address: www.newharbinger.com

04 03 02

10 9 8 7 6 5 4 3 2 1

First printing

For my husband David
with all my love

Contents

Part Four
Putting It All Together and Living Your Life

Foreword

One of the most rewarding experiences for a teacher is the discovery of a gifted student. Dr. Stefanie Stolinsky, from the beginning, has proved to be one of those delightful discoveries.

As my former student, who has become a successful psychologist, she brings to our profession a unique perspective. Utilizing her background and training as an actor, combined with her training as a psychologist, Dr. Stolinsky has innovated a series of acting exercises that encourage victims of childhood abuse to begin a process of self-healing. This process is much more powerful than simply remembering and recounting those earlier events. It provides the individual with an emotional pathway to forever exorcize the pent-up pain that controls so much of that person's adult existence.

Act It Out offers the reader an opportunity to travel beyond an intellectual understanding of their struggle to become a more integrated, self-loving person. These exercises assist in the release of the deeper, more unconscious feelings that mold a lifestyle devoted to convincing themselves and others that they are doing fine even as they continue to feel the sadness, fear, anger, and insecurities that haunt so many victims of childhood trauma. Written with compassion and respect, *Act It Out* invites the reader to privately begin to release old sensations that feed feelings of shame and self-doubt.

For many who read this book it will open new doors to the possibility of beginning the journey to create the satisfying lifestyle they deserve. For others it may offer the finishing touch to a journey already begun. Wherever each person stands on the path to overcoming, they now have a companion and a guide to lead them safely into that place of self-healing where the light of emotional release forever illumines the dark corners of the cave and scatters unconscious fears that have imprisoned their capacity for fully realizing their own potential and reaping the benefits of their inspiring acts of courage

—Trudy Moss, Ph.D.

Preface

In the *Los Angeles Times*, Monday, June 4, 2001, obituary of Academy Award–winner Anthony Quinn, the author quoted Quinn as saying that he only came to grips with his first son's death in a drowning accident forty years ago when Quinn played Zorba in *Zorba the Greek*. Zorba, too, had lost a son. Quinn reported that every night doing the show, he had to say, "He's dead." That helped Quinn deal with and overcome the pain he had felt for so many years.

In the book *Acting for Real* (Emunah 1994), author Renee Emunah quotes actor Marlon Brando as saying, "Acting has done as much as anything to make me realize my violence and get rid of it. And when I finished *The Wild Ones* [a motion picture] I think it was gone forever."

Jacob L. Moreno, M.D. (1889-1974) was credited as the founder of psychodrama, a therapy technique which enabled clients to use spontaneity and creativity to enact situations dramatically in different kinds of therapy: family, individual, or group. Psychodrama focused on specific problems of individuals, unlike drama therapy, which focused more generally on developing spontaneity and self-awareness.

Different techniques were used in both psychodrama and drama therapy. Most notably, role-playing helped clients in psychodrama gain the ability to explore inner pain while working it out on a "stage" (Corsisni and Wedding 1989).

However, throughout history, from shamanic to modern day religions and cultures, problems both mental and physical have been reenacted, the feelings reexamined, and healing has taken place. In fact, various forms of drama have been used throughout history to help people deal with psychic pain (Ellenberger 1970).

One of the most potent and valuable ways of working toward understanding yourself and how you created your own personality through your life experiences is to reenact some of the moments, sounds, sights, objects, and feelings connected to experiences that contributed to the formation of *you*. These memories of experiences will allow you to unfold the amazing creation that is your mind, talent, and potential for success.

Acknowledgments

My father was a motion-picture producer and a writer, and my mother was a professional oil painter. My husband, David, a retired medical oncologist, is also doing extremely well as an essayist. So I am more than well aware of the collaboration it takes to realize any work of art. I have so many wonderful friends and colleagues to thank for helping me with this book.

First and foremost, I would like to thank my wonderful husband, David, for reading and rereading this manuscript with love and devotion to every detail. I want to thank my parents for supporting and loving me when they were alive. I want to thank my friend, Sylvia Cary, MFT "editor extrordinaire," who has stood behind me all the way, with love, advice, devotion, and stamina rarely seen in anyone. She pushed me to keep going and not to get caught up in the little things. Thank you so much.

Also first, I want to thank Carole Honeychurch, M.A., at New Harbinger for being an absolutely brilliant diagnostician and editing guru. What a talented, amazing lady! Her respect, knowledge, and editing ability were incredible during this entire process.

Thanks especially to all my clients. I've learned so much from all of you.

I want to thank Trudy Moss, Ph.D., Donna Sexsmith, Ph.D., Terry Oleson, Ph.D., Susan Murphy, Ph.D., Nancy Kezlarian, MFT, Carole Disnehof, Ph.D., and Kara Cross, Ph.D. and all my friends and colleagues who gave me so much support during the ten years off and on that it took me to complete this work. Thanks for standing by me, and thanks for all your stories and case reports that helped me organize and realize my thoughts and put them on paper.

I also want to thank my friend, Robert Mulcahy, Esq., who was ready and able to give me legal advice and pushed me to keep up the work.

And thanks to Gussie, my Airedale terrier, for sitting endlessly by my side during the long hours I spent at th computer.

I feel that if this book can help even one person out there to work on their child-abuse issues enough to prevent themselves from ruining a perfectly good, full-of-potential relationship in order to look for some nonexistent, fantasy relationship that they think might be better or more or different than what they have at home, I have done my job. If you have a good relationship, one that can grow and be nurtured, work on that to the best of your ability. If it really isn't what you want, then leave it and begin anew with a fresh knowledge of who you are and what you want.

Part One

Why Acting Exercises?

Chapter 1

A Therapist's Legacy

On New Year's Day, 1996, my friend Sandy, a therapist and colleague, was found dead in the hills of Angeles National Forest. She had killed herself three days earlier by downing a bottle of Seconal with a bottle of vodka, but her body wasn't found until someone bicycling in the area spotted her slumped over in her car.

Her death had been preceded by years of physical and sexual abuse by her father, uncles, brothers, and boyfriends. She had never experienced a relationship in which she felt safe and loved. She had been used as a sexual object for as long as she could remember.

Sandy had spent most of her adult life in and out of therapy and was only too familiar with all of the various therapies available: psychodynamic, cognitive-behavioral, family, psychodrama, and others. She had gone from one therapist to another in what seemed to be a futile attempt to find an end to her pain. She wanted to find out why her relationships were always stormy and why she was unable to trust anyone. In the end, she took to her grave all the memories, conscious and unconscious, that had filled her life with fear, emptiness, and hopelessness.

Sandy's current boyfriend absolved himself of any participation in the reasons for her death. He was an elusive, emotionally unavailable fellow who complained to Sandy that she was "too needy" and that he couldn't stand her hanging on to him so tightly. When I heard about Sandy's death, I was stunned. How could this woman, who understood more about child abuse than anyone I knew—this woman who had sought out every treatment available to heal herself—end up committing suicide? What went wrong? It preyed on my mind.

Memories of Sandy, a sensitive, beautiful, compassionate young woman, flooded back to me. I had first met her in 1988 when I was a a psychology student at UCLA. I was still learning about the subject of child abuse and was in the process of working on a UCLA study, developing a questionnaire for therapists to hand out to their clients. Sandy helped me with this questionnaire, even filled it out herself, giving me pointers and guidance all along the way. I was impressed with the depth of her understanding of people who were in psychic pain.

When Sandy told me the details of her own sexual abuse history, her story touched me deeply. Her father, a well-known actor, had begun fondling her genitals when she was still in the crib. As she became a toddler, she slapped his hands away. Then he would beat her. The abuse progressed until Sandy was in high school and became pregnant by her father. This pregnancy precipitated the immediate divorce of her parents. Sandy had the child, a boy, who was brain damaged. She was told that he would be dead within three years. She gave the child up for adoption.

Her father then left the home, and Sandy found herself in a series of relationships with men who were brutal emotionally and often physically. Her relationships never lasted longer than three months, and no matter how they began, they ended with her either being beaten up or abandoned (usually with rent money due), suffering tears and confusion about what went wrong *this* time. She always maintained that she was searching for love but never knew what it looked or felt like.

Despite all the turmoil in her life, she managed to graduate from college in the top 10 percent of her class and then earned a Ph.D. in child psychology. During her schooling, she remained in therapy four times a week. When that didn't work as well as she had anticipated, she changed the type of therapy and began keeping journals, but that proved to be too threatening; she didn't know what to do with all that writing.

In spite of all her intellectual knowledge and expertise, and in spite of all the therapy she'd had, she was never able to fully heal from the long-term effects of her early child abuse.

In the end, child abuse killed her. How could such a thing happen?

The shock of my friend's death became the reason that I ended up writing my Ph.D. dissertation on the subject of child abuse, and, after having spent a number of years as a working actress, ultimately ended up working as a psychotherapist in this field. Along the way, I developed a new method of treating child abuse survivors in therapy by using formal acting techniques and exercises. And it is because of the success I have achieved with these exercises that I have written this book.

I was fortunate to have Sandy and other excellent teachers, supervisors, mentors, colleagues, and friends who all contributed to this book. I owe them a lot.

What Is Child Abuse?

Simply put, child abuse is the exploitation of or assault on a child. It can be verbal, emotional, physical, or sexual. The different types of child abuse can overlap. For example, any time a child is sexually abused (touched in a sexual way, penetrated, or subjected to fellatio), that child has, by definition, also been physically and emotionally abused. The child has also been emotionally abused if he or she watched another child being treated in these ways.

Some literature has denied long-term aftereffects for all survivors, but most children who have suffered abuse have scars from it.

Up until the late 1960s, the whole subject of child abuse was a hush-hush thing, a subject pretty much swept under the rug. Therapists were uncomfortable with it, and victims of abuse, feeling shame along with a whole host of other emotions, cooperated by keeping silent. It was all a big secret.

Then, in 1968, child-abuse reporting laws began to hit the books. Mental health and medical personnel nationwide began to be required by law to report any incident of child abuse they heard about in their offices. This law forced mental-health professionals across the board, many of whom had been ignoring the child-abuse phenomenon, to make it their business to learn more about it, and not just about the various categories of abuse, but about the whole range of aftereffects that last long after the abuse itself is over.

Today, child abuse is a topic that's out in the open. The statistics are astounding. An estimated three million children a year are affected. Approximately three children die each day from the results of abuse or neglect. While other crime rates seem to be falling, the incidence of child abuse is growing and is becoming one of the nation's most critical public health issues.

At least today we have all kinds of excellent information available to us. Therapists, by law, must get special training in child abuse in order to keep up their professional licenses. There are nonprofit groups specializing in child abuse all over the country. There are help hotlines. The media has done numerous programs, educating the public. And, thanks to the Internet, there are hundreds of child-abuse related Web sites, lists of organizations, and chat-lines where abuse victims can communicate with each other and get additional information. There are also community self-help groups for abuse survivors, and one online bookstore lists nearly 2,700 books on the subject.

Three Basic Categories of Abuse

There are three basic categories of abuse: emotional (verbal) abuse; physical abuse; and sexual abuse.

Emotional (Verbal) Abuse

Name-calling, belittling, humiliation, irrational blaming, insults, threatening behavior, embarrassing a child, cruel teasing, presenting "double binds" (contradictory rules), purposely frightening a child, or making remarks of a suggestive or sexual nature constitute emotional abuse. Sticks and stones may break your bones and names do hurt you. For a child, verbal and emotional abuse is absolutely devastating. A child who is left neglected in the hope "someone" will watch out for him or her is another example of emotional abuse.

Just recently I witnessed an example of verbal child abuse in a bookstore. A woman, there with her little girl, was calling the child names and putting her down in a loud voice just for asking questions. Finally, the child said to her, "Mom, why are you so mean to me?" at which point the mother began yelling at her all over again for talking back to her.

Another time, I heard a woman call her daughter "a big horse" when the child was hungry and ate too much for lunch. These emotional assaults cut deep, can linger, and can end up with the emotionally abused child turning into an angry, vengeful adult in later relationships.

Secrecy is also a form of emotional child abuse.

My friend Glenda was lied to consistently in childhood. She never learned of her mother's potentially devastating breast cancer because in those days no one ever talked seriously to a child about adult matters. Consequently, during the illness, when Glenda saw her mother grieving or sorrowful, the child thought she had caused the problem that made the mother so sad. Glenda grew up feeling she was a bad person, someone who had let her mother down. Only later did she find out the truth of her mother's illness and that she could be not to blame. But the damage was done. Glenda once told her mother she never wanted to love or trust anyone because it was too dangerous. Only after learning through exercises who she was and how giving and loving she could be, did she begin to trust herself.

Fortunately, in adulthood she did find love, and learned to trust many friends, thanks to her emotional recovery. This recovery came about in an unusual way: through the acting exercises that she learned when she was training to be an actress. As it turned out, it was these acting exercises, not formal personal psychotherapy, that enabled her to get in touch with the fear, guilt, and helplessness that were a result of the emotional abuse she had experienced as a child.

Physical Abuse

Physical abuse consists of hitting, beating, punching, or otherwise attacking a child bodily. One of the first clients I saw in a hospital setting was Charles, a sixty-five-year-old man with dissociative disorder who had been physically abused by his father. When Charles was only five or six years old, his father, who was considered to be a bully in the neighborhood, tortured him by putting him in a bathtub and running hot water over him. Then his father put electrical cords in the water, causing sparks that almost electrocuted the boy. Although Charles' IQ was later found to be close to "genius," he developed his serious dissociative disorder as the result of those years of physical torture and abuse. He was in and out of mental institutions for most of his life.

Today, even spankings, shaking, and other forms of physical disciplines and punishments are considered physical abuse. Researchers and therapists have often described how physical beatings can become sexualized in the victim's mind. A child who is being hit, beaten, or strapped might find that this aggression leads to sexual feelings (Freud 1938). This kind of connection can trigger an unhealthy association between sexuality and pain for the rest of the person's life.

In his book, *Social Psychology* (1987), author David Meyers has shown that children who are hit or beaten often end up hitting or beating their elders when the latter are old and in need of someone to care for them. In therapy, clients often complain that their parents, who may look old and feeble now, used to beat them mercilessly when they were young. These resentments can fester, and in adulthood, the victims may seek revenge.

Sexual Abuse

Sexual abuse means the exploitation of, or sexual assault on any child under the age of eighteen. It is now a crime for a therapist or other mental or medical practitioner *not* to file a report with the Department of Child Protective Services if they suspect or know about a child being subjected to pornography or to assault (which means touching, licking, penetration by digits or sex organs, exposing one's self, or talking suggestively to a child). Sexual abuse is the form of child abuse that most victims, as well as most perpetrators, try to keep secret—which makes it worse.

Child Abuse is *Not* "Cured" by Reaching Adulthood

The main thing I learned from working with Sandy, from my studies in child abuse over the years, and from my therapeutic work with survivors of child abuse is that the aftereffects of abuse don't go away when the victim grows up (Beitchman et al. 1992). The symptoms linger on painfully and negatively affect every area of the survivor's life. Sweeping the reality of the abuse under the rug doesn't work either. Denying it doesn't work. Minimizing it doesn't work. Trying not to think about it doesn't work.

The only thing that works is dealing with it head on.

Child abuse, be it emotional, physical, or sexual, always packs a punch. For the rest of their lives, survivors walk around with free-floating feelings of anger, anxiety, or fear and often don't even know where all these feelings are coming from.

Some survivors find it particularly difficult to reveal and describe exactly what happened to them as children. They are filled with feelings of shame, humiliation, and self-blame. They want to hide the truth. Many opt to escape into fantasy lives instead of working out their past trauma in therapy. They become "actors" in their own lives without really living *their* life.

Trust, which develops in the first stage of childhood, is a crucial issue for survivors of childhood abuse. Children who learn they cannot trust their parents and caregivers (because they were abused by them) later have trouble trusting anyone else. Anytime they begin to feel even the semblance of trust coming on, they may quickly close off any emotion, sure that others will misuse their trust and ultimately let them down. This mistrust extends to their therapists as well. Survivors often flit from therapist to therapist, never satisfied or content that they have found out anything they hadn't already discovered for themselves. They get stuck in patterns of self-doubt, low-esteem, and self-sabotage, resistant to change yet angry and full of despair over staying in the same place.

Abuse survivors often find themselves physically acting out their emotions in unsuitable ways and with inappropriate people. Stealing, fighting, angry outbursts, self-destructive behaviors, and addictions are typical of abuse survivors. Only a structured, definite treatment geared to interrupting these destructive behaviors and getting survivors back on track will enable them to recover from the abuse and lead normal, satisfying lives.

Discovering "Acting Exercises" as Treatment

The more I worked as a psychotherapist with the survivors of child abuse, the more convinced I became that therapy, to be effective, needed some new dimension to it. To me, the fact of Sandy's death was proof that what already existed wasn't enough. Something else needed to be added to the mix.

As I mentioned above, that "something else" turned out to be acting exercises—the very same acting exercises used by actors and actresses in drama schools and classes to help them improve their acting skills and land better roles. These acting exercises can also help child-abuse survivors land better and happier "roles" in life by helping them uncover, slowly and under their control, feelings from their pasts.

I knew about these acting exercises because, before I became a psychotherapist, I spent fifteen years as an actress. I studied with some of the top acting teachers, including Lee Strasberg of The Actor's Studio, Stella Adler, and Bobby Lewis, so I had learned some of the best acting techniques in the world. I also taught acting.

Later, after I switched careers and began working with child-abuse survivors, I began to notice that many of my clients presented the same kinds of complaints and impasses in their therapy sessions as did many actors and actresses in their drama classes. For example, actors often have difficulty releasing emotions (such as sadness, weakness, or tears) for fear of being thought of as "too much" or going "over the top." They feel constrained and stop themselves; they play it safe. If they do hold back, they may end up losing the role to someone else because releasing true emotion when it is called for is what acting is all about.

In therapy, abuse survivors do the same thing. They hide, hold back, fear being themselves or expressing their feelings, and end up losing relationships in their lives that are important to them because they don't know how to be "real."

Because of these striking similarities between the dynamics of actors and those of abuse survivors, I began incorporating acting exercises into my therapy sessions, reasoning that if acting exercises can help actors get unblocked, then acting exercises should also be able to help get abuse survivors unblocked.

Lisa's Story

I started with Lisa, a woman who came to see me for therapy after she had been brutally beaten by her boyfriend. Her guilt and depression were so profound that she could not function at work, where she was an executive secretary to a CEO of a very big tire firm. She'd go into work with bandages and give phony explanations about falling off her motorcycle. Her coworkers were naturally skeptical. In therapy, she was unable to express how angry and betrayed she felt. We talked for six months, and each week she'd be just as depressed and unhappy as she had been the week before. Even though I encouraged her to talk, she couldn't. She was hopelessly blocked. She would sit until the hour was up, then pay me, thank me, and leave. Sometimes I was sure she would never come back, but the next week, there she'd be, and we'd go through the whole thing again.

People who have experienced abuse in childhood are often afraid that their "secret" might come out, and they will forever be branded as dirty or used. It's too hard to verbalize what happened. Secrecy is probably just what happened during the actual abuse. Child-abuse survivors are often told by their abusers not to tell anyone, keep the secret—or else. But the body remembers, and this keeping secrets is just like "holding back" for an actor.

Much in the same way the body reacts during surgery, when, although you are under anesthesia, the body knows it is being cut, sewn up, or whatever, the body "remembers" abuse, hurt, or pain by reacting in adulthood in the same way it reacted during the abuse. The problem is that now a person may actually *desire* to be touched, fondled, and loved, but their body only remembers that this is frightening, dangerous, or painful and will retract in the same way it did when abuse occurred. This explains why certain touches feel familiar even though you may believe consciously that you have never experienced them—the unconscious remembers. That is why it is so important to make the unconscious conscious. Once you know where and how these uncomfortable feelings got started, you can begin to separate those emotions from your adult emotions now.

One day I asked Lisa to try the Empty Chair exercise, borrowed from Gestalt therapy. She put an imaginary person in an empty chair and spoke to that person as if they were really sitting there. But halfway through the exercise Lisa clammed up. Another week, I asked her to write down her feelings in a journal. That didn't work either. I was beginning to think about referring Lisa to another counselor, when during what I thought might be our last session, I asked her if she would like to try just one more tactic—an acting exercise I had used at the Actor's Institute called the Coffee Cup Exercise.

I shared this exercise with Lisa, because it was active and action-oriented, and I thought it might help her unleash some of the feelings that were so locked up inside her. I asked her to hold out her hand, palm up, and imagine putting an object, any object, into that hand. It didn't have to be a coffee cup, but it should be a familiar object that she was involved with every day. It could be small (like a button), medium (like a coffee cup), or even something "large," like a miniature rendition of her home.

Lisa studied her open palm for a moment, and then, suddenly, some large tears formed in her eyes and slid down her face. She didn't speak. She brought her hands very close to her face and began to stroke whatever she was holding. Then she said, "My best friend I had as a child was my dog, Bow." And, imagining holding her dog's face in her hand, Lisa began telling her story of being a slave to two alcoholic, fighting parents who used her like a servant. She cleaned the house, made the meals, cleaned up their vomit, and took care of the younger children, a boy, six months, and a girl, three. She was kept home from school many weeks at a time to cater to their needs.

Her dog had been a silent witness to her childhood slavery. But he, too, had suffered at the hands of her father, who , when he was drunk, used to throw the animal against a wall. Lisa had saved the dog's life by secretly hiding him in a suitcase that had been punched with three air holes for the poor animal to breathe. When the family went on their next trip to visit Lisa's grandmother, who lived far away, Lisa left the suitcase in her grandmother's living room. Her grandmother had loved her, and she kept the dog, but she'd been powerless to help Lisa get away from the brutality.

As she told me the story of her childhood, Lisa immediately began to feel as if a great burden had been lifted. She said, "I'm so glad to finally tell someone and get this off my back." In the weeks that followed, we used more and more acting exercises: the Shower Exercise to reconnect her mind with her body, the Portrait Exercise to help her realize her identity, and a Sense Memory to remember her grandmother's love. Sometimes we would use each exercise alone and sometimes in combination, and she continued to improve and feel better.

Each exercise Lisa did seemed to open up another forgotten door and help her find important lost memories and the feelings that went along with them. Some memories made her feel angry and sad; others worried her but increased her recall. However, because she finally felt safe enough within the structure of each exercise to express her feelings, she found she experienced each emotion fully and completely.

Emotional Hierarchy

Lisa's case was just the beginning. As I used the acting exercises approach with other abuse patients, I began to see that there is a hierarchical way of working that allows people to open up slowly yet at their own pace, which gives them back much of the control they felt they had lost as the result of their sexual, physical, or emotional abuse. And, even though I knew that art therapy, Gestalt therapy, and some forms of psychodrama appear to aid in expression, I still believed that they put too many demands on the client. Simply offering up exercises alone would be a deciding factor in helping trauma survivors find their voices.

Acting Exercises as Psychotherapy

I also began to discover that acting exercises are a useful adjunct in psychotherapy, even for clients who haven't experienced child abuse. Today, I use acting exercises with great results all the time, not only with abuse survivors, but with any client who wishes to see the arc of their life. Most of these exercises can be done at home, alone, and without a teacher or therapist present.

All the acting exercises that follow in this book are those I either learned in acting classes or have personally developed by observing how my clients (and how actors) pay attention to their wants and needs. The exercises have turned out to be a major contribution in helping many survivors of abuse unleash emotion in the same way actors utilize them to better understand and develop their characters.

So let's sum up the reasons for using acting exercises to heal abuse:

Ten Reasons to Use Acting Exercises to Heal Child Abuse

1. **Acting exercises offer hope.** Hope creates purpose, and that is the one thing that never lets us down in life—the need to always be doing something positive and action-oriented to feel alive.

2. **Acting exercises help make the unconscious conscious.** Many of our problems are hidden behind defenses, so exposing a feeling or need may appear frightening at first. By systematically opening up our unconscious mind to consciousness, we can capture and control the memories of lost feelings and de-escalate the power they have over our adult lives.

3. **Acting exercises help you discover your autonomous "true self."** By using acting exercises, you uncover your identity. No longer are there other people to tell you who you "should" be, or who you are. You are in the process of uncovering, for yourself, your true feelings.

4. **Acting exercises help you find spontaneity and build trust.** Acting, by definition, is creating. When we create from our intuition, working moment to moment, we build spontaneity. That, in turn, allows us to trust our creative process. What we have created is part of our whole being, and we can trust that what we find is who we are, not part of someone else.

5. **Acting exercises are a safe way to remember and feel.** As one acting teacher I had warned, we cannot eat an entire turkey, we need to cut off pieces and then make bite-sized pieces of the portion on our plates. The same is true for the unconscious. We need to help it evolve in a way that does not overwhelm us or make us stop too soon for fear of what we might find. Acting exercises give that kind of control over inner emotional states.

6. **Acting exercises help you become more creative in your recovery.** Creativity enables you to find more insights, which in turn will lead to your control over the aftereffects of your trauma. Once you have insights, you have a choice—you can continue to respond the way you always have to particular problems, or you can make a deliberate decision to alter your responses to be more adaptive to your life now.

7. **Acting exercises can give you success right now.** Acting has the positive aspect of being immediate. As you discover how your own creativity and ability enable you to find new and energized ways of dealing with your trauma, you will also notice how your recovery time is shortened substantially by the spontaneity of your efforts. This spontaneity further enhances your belief in your own powers to take control over the effects of your trauma. As you finish each exercise, you will feel rewarded and empowered by your inner strength and talents.

8. **Acting exercises help you act, not "act out."** "Acting out" means being out of control—lashing out verbally in traffic or hitting, punching, or attacking someone or something. Any acting out behavior as opposed to speaking out behavior can be damaging to you, often making you feel weak. Instead, you do want to act, but act by recreating events and objects in your life to help you heal and give you a voice and language with which to speak out your concerns.

9. **Acting exercises help you make the mind/body connection.** Your body holds all the memories and pain of your abuse. But, by enabling yourself to use objects to trigger forgotten experiences, you use your mind and your body together to emotionally and physically heal from them.

10. **Acting exercises are fun.** So many words describe acting: empowering, enlightening, exciting, enabling, and fruitful are just a few. But imagine the heightened feeling you will have when you're able to be yourself in the real world.

Sandy's Legacy

So, as I grieve for Sandy to this day, I am also grateful for her legacy. Because of her and other survivors, I have been able to develop a treatment for overcoming the aftereffects of child abuse that, had she lived, might even have been able to help her. We'll never know, although I like to think it would. What I do know for sure is that these acting exercises have definitely helped many other survivors like Sandy learn how to find a way to take control of their lives and deal with the effects of their abuse. I know that is what Sandy wanted so very much for herself.

Now let's move on to chapter 2, looking at the many and varied symptoms and aftereffects of childhood abuse.

Chapter 2

Aftermath: Symptoms from A to Z

Do you have good relationships? Do you have a solid, long-lasting work history? Do you find that your friendships last, or do they come and go?

What's your "communication style"? Are you able to accept responsibility for your feelings and actions, or are you a blamer? Do you think that most of your pain has been caused by somebody else—that your problems are really somebody else's fault?

Do you walk around with free-floating anger? Always being negative about yourself and constantly looking for the negative in others?

Do you find that when a new friend comes into your life, at first you love them, everything about them seems perfect, but then, after a while, little things—a word, a gesture—begin to irk you and cause you to begin to devalue them? Suddenly they're not as special as you initially thought. You begin to worry that you can't trust your intuition about your relationships after all. Perhaps you promised yourself that you would never act like one of your parents, and then you find yourself reacting to things just as they did. You try to be the opposite of a parent—only to realize that the very fact that you have to be so *different* is in itself proof of the power they still have over you. You can't seem to be who *you* really are.

Perhaps, deep inside, you know that you could do more with your life. You know how much you have to give to others and to yourself. You know what would make you happy, and you know what would make you more successful. So what's in your way?

What's Stopping You?

While most people, even those who are fortunate enough not to have been abused in childhood, can identify with *some* of these "symptoms," when it gets to the point where you identify with many or most of them, then childhood abuse, remembered or not, should be considered.

The Impact of Aftereffects

Certain personality characteristics show up consistently in the survivors of emotional, physical, and/or sexual abuse in childhood. The scars that are left present themselves in a variety of ways. For every action, there's a reaction. That's a law of physics. It's also a law of human nature.

The aftereffects of traumas you experienced as a child can pop up at any time and get in the way of your success and happiness today. They can visit you and mess with you in every single aspect of your life, even when you try to sweep them under the carpet. Just when you start thinking you have things under control, even a minor situation on the outside can trigger a major reaction inside. Or maybe you've gone to the other extreme—to the point where you can't even feel when you *want* to. You've managed to numb yourself. You feel nothing.

Aftereffects can pop up in unconscious as well as conscious ways—such as during sex. A sexually numb woman (because of earlier abuse) may fake orgasms to make her partner feel good about himself, but then feel angry and sexually impoverished herself, often to the point of taking it out on him at a later date.

How Do You Heal from All These Destructive Symptoms and Patterns?

First, before you can treat them, you have to learn what they are, what they're called, what they look like, and how they may be affecting you. For this you'll need some guidance, just as actors need guidance to become successful artists.

Let's start by taking a look at some of the typical symptoms or aftereffects of abuse in childhood. Some, you'll notice, overlap. Along the way, I will mention some of the acting exercises that I use and recommend for dealing with specific symptoms—exercises that I will discuss in detail in part 2 of this book.

Aftereffects of Childhood Abuse A–Z

These are some of the major symptoms that can make up the aftereffects of your abuse.

Alienation

You consistently alienate others by doing things and saying things that push them away. You may reveal a friend's secrets, or even use certain words you know will upset them and cause them to withdraw. Knowing that will happen doesn't seem to deter you from doing it or saying it anyway.

George, a fifty-six-year-old traffic school teacher, a man who had been emotionally abused as a child, had lost jobs as an RN, a technician in a hospital, and as a computer programmer because he constantly insulted coworkers. He couldn't seem to stop. Even his divorce from his wife of ten years was a direct result of his telling a group of people intimate details about their sex life, including the fact that she was "frigid." He knew better, but he couldn't seem to stop his mouth. He ended up alienating everyone. He even announced to his class at the traffic school, "Before this day is over, someone here will hate me."

George couldn't bear intimacy so he actively pushed people away. Nor could he voice his resentment over the fact that when he was a teenager, he had to support his mother and four brothers and sisters. He missed out on a social life, a career in medicine, and ultimately ended up in the army. He couldn't remember a single day in his youth when he'd been happy.

In therapy with George, I utilized a technique called the Gibberish Exercise where I directed him to say whatever he wanted out loud but in gibberish, something like the nonsense language many of us made up and used as kids. As he began working on this exercise, his anger and frustration came out in full force. Where he couldn't seem to find the words to speak out his pain because as he put it, "I'm not a wimp," the Gibberish Exercise allowed him a transitional period in which to feel the experience without being required to speak about it in English. With this technique he concentrated on his feelings. Ultimately, he was able to verbally recount them in English, and then contain them.

Anger

Are you an angry person? Has anger hurt your relationships or your business more than once? Do you find that your first response to anything problematic is anger? Do you wish you could control your anger but find that it's controlling you instead?

Many of my clients describe feeling "out of control" with their anger. Almost anything can set them off. Anger that comes from child abuse is usually fragmented. That is, many different and seemingly unconnected abuses probably made you angry originally, and after a while they all seem to meld together. In fact, you probably can't even remember what the primary situation was that started your rage, but your anger probably grew and multiplied. You may even notice that even now that you are actively seeking answers, the anger doesn't seem to dissipate.

As you apply a number of acting exercises to your anger, you will be able to bring in the reins and uncover exactly what first made you so angry. You will also find how you can control your rage effectively.

Avoiding

Avoiding is a form of escape and may be an indication of your inability to trust yourself with other people. You may be avoiding others for fear of being rejected, being ridiculed, or perhaps you have never been able to open up to being part of a group. You may tell yourself you're not a "people person." But avoidant behavior has been described as *hiding* behavior because the person doing the avoiding is, at the root of it, afraid that he or she is not perfect. Avoiders describe giving up ever trying to fit in because they can't be perfect. When survivors realize that avoiding will never work, they become ashamed of being avoidant. And that makes the problem a vicious cycle.

Abuse survivors often become avoidant personalities, and their avoidant behavior can make them quite depressed. Clients who have suffered being alone for fear of "never doing anything right" often believe that whatever they do will be found out by "the authorities" to be wrong. Oddly, many of these clients can never tell me exactly who these authorities are. But, fearing embarrassment, these survivors will do things like dropping out of society by taking a hidden job where they can work in the middle of the night when no one is around. That way, there's no one nearby who can further shame them.

With the Eye to Eye exercise in part 3 you will silently "stare" someone right in the eye for as long as you can without averting your gaze. In this way, the exercise can be a tool to help you eliminate your avoidance tactics. As you look directly into someone else's eyes, you will discover that you can get in touch with your own primary emotions quickly. That connection with your real feelings will enable you to communicate emotions nonverbally. Initially, you may find yourself laughing or even crying. But you will soon find that these initial reactions give way to your imparting concrete information to someone, and you may notice that other emotions that have previously prevented honest communication, such as humiliation or embarrassment, are gone.

Blame

One way abuse survivors try to gain control in their adult lives is to blame themselves for their child abuse. You may feel you were forced or cajoled into doing things your instincts told you were "wrong"—but are you now blaming yourself for causing the abuse to happen? You shouldn't be. It's never your fault; it's *always* the abuser's fault. So why do we blame ourselves?

Many therapists say blaming yourself is a way to gain control over the abuse. A lot of survivors were told later by their nonabusive parent or even their abusers that they had control over the abuse incident. Some were convinced by their perpetrators that they actually *wanted* to be abused.

One of my clients told me her father rationalized, "All fathers do this with their daughters." She grew up feeling, "If only I hadn't been so seductive." Other survivors have lamented, "If only I had locked my bedroom door," then perhaps they would have controlled or even stopped what happened. Many of these survivors convince themselves that they were to blame because they became excited or had orgasms. Because of this, they rationalize that the abuse really was under their control and, therefore, must be their fault.

You may be using blame to exact punishment for yourself. So, how can you, a survivor of child abuse, forgive yourself for any excitement you felt, find peace in the here and now, and know that no one is allowed to abuse you now? Survivors find it hard to believe that *child abuse is always the perpetrator's fault.* But hearing it intellectually is often the first time they can begin to feel it emotionally. So, hear it again and try to remember, *the abuser is always to blame.*

An exercise that addresses this question is the "Put Your Partner on a Pedestal Exercise" in which two people gain the truth by problem-solving together, and techniques come into play that tease out truth from fiction and help the players end the exercise.

Cheating

Cheating others is a way for survivors to feel they are "getting even" for all the iniquities done to them. It's payback time. If they can't exact their pound of flesh, it's a kind of retribution or vindication. They are getting even with the world.

Amelia was an excellent student and knew the information weeks before an exam, but she still had an addictive need to cheat on tests in school. "I wrote out an entire five pages from a textbook one time and simply inserted it into the examination book. The professor gave me an A because he was so impressed that I had been able to 'memorize' all that. I laughed myself sick." But Amelia's real excitement came from finding new ways of never being detected in her cheating. The problem was, her grades were never really her own, and ultimately she *couldn't keep up with the work in the major she had chosen.*

The As If Exercise helped her define what she truly felt she had been cheated out of as a child and how she might find appropriate ways to get her wants and needs met now.

Control Problems

Small children cannot stand the thought of a "bad" adult. It goes against everything they need to believe in order to be safe as a kid. They depend on adults for food, clothing, shelter, care, protection, and nurturing. So when anything bad happens that is, at least to the rest of us, clearly the adult's fault, the child puts all that blame on himself or herself in an attempt to keep the adult idealized. This idealization can continue into adulthood when the adult survivor continues to take the responsibility for anything that goes wrong in order to keep the other person squeaky clean. In that way a survivor can actually feel they are in control of all subsequent situations.

One way survivors try to get out of the feeling of being "trapped" by the abuse, or believe they will prevent future abuse, is to say to themselves or someone else, "I will take control. I will never allow this to happen to me again."

From that point forward, they try to anticipate, notice, and be on top of everything that comes their way—an exhausting, if not impossible, job.

Denying

Denying is a form of lying. Both are part of the same dynamic because both are pretending—pretending that the abuse didn't happen. I've been shocked more than once by how people, especially perpetrators, use denial to convince themselves they did nothing wrong. In fact, to them, nothing happened at all. Sometimes the victim is as adamant as the abuser in denying a transgression.

A movie producer I knew demonstrated typical denial tactics. He apparently couldn't confront his promiscuity. He had an image of himself that was above cheating on his wife and compromising his family. But he still came on sexually to every woman he met, actress or not. And even though he ended up in bed with as many women as he could, he maintained that he was completely faithful to his wife!

One actress accused him of using her sexually by promising her a part in a film if she'd sleep with him, a well-known "casting couch" practice. I don't think she was actually surprised by his deception, but she sure was shocked by his reply. When she confronted him, he adamantly denied ever having sex with her. His serious response was, "We never did anything." It was as if a part of his brain had completely split off from the other parts and contained or held knowledge that he couldn't stand to admit. Some murderers employ the very same tactic.

Many abuse survivors also build up an elaborate set of rationalizations for what happened to them. Carla, a twenty-eight-year-old computer programmer, reported that when she was four years old, her mother used to position her on the kitchen table to douche her "private parts," allowing the entire family to watch as if Carla were the star of a "show." The shame and humiliation Carla suffered during these intrusive baths was so severe that she later managed to convince herself that nothing untoward had really happened. Instead, she chastised herself for having a filthy, dirty mind and told herself that *that* was why these memories were so threatening and disgusting to her.

Because of her childhood abuse, Carla began to act out her anger in her teens. In her mind, she had caused the abuse to occur—so she deserved to be punished. She began allowing older men to become sexual with her and began referring to herself as "the tramp of high school."

Depression

Lingering, long-term depression is one of the most resistant aftereffects of child abuse because it can feel so broad. Many things during the day can depress you: low energy, malaise, lack of interest and lack of desire to take action even on your own behalf. Many survivors can feel like those poor animals in "learned helplessness" experiments taught in every psychology program. A bunny is put on a grid and then prevented from leaving the grid during electrical shocks. When the rabbit is finally permitted to leave the grid, it won't—because it has learned to feel helpless. It remains on the grid and takes the abuse. This inability to escape causes long-term depression, which takes many years to abate, if ever.

Abuse survivors find it almost impossible to be happy and relieved of the memories of their trauma. They live in constant fear and sadness that these memories will dominate their minds and encroach on every relationship they try to have.

Eating Disorders

Eating disorders have gotten a lot of attention lately—many books, articles, and talk shows are focused on what they mean, what they hide, and what helps overcome them. For child abuse survivors, eating disorders are just another way to push down feelings connected with the abuse, as well as an indication that the person is unable to trust. Food temporarily loves you, so you can forget your pain for the moment and enjoy yourself. But each pound you put on just represents the agony you felt as a child. As an adult, you're continuing to feel that agony.

Although many reasons have been put forth as "causing" eating disorders, abuse survivors often describe their eating problems, especially overweight issues, as unresolved anger. The survivor wants to be big enough to push abusers and would-be abusers away. Other survivors are convinced that as long as they are overweight, they are punishing their bodies for responding to the abuse or even allowing it to have occurred. Often eating disorders poorly mask the desire for control.

Acting exercises can help you work through your anxiety and depression without taking it out on your body. You will be using your body to recreate permanent good feelings. That will help you discover your own power to heal without resorting to outside substances, including food, alcohol, drugs, or addictive destructive behaviors to temporarily feel good about yourself.

Fear

Trauma victims usually experience a type of fear associated with post-traumatic stress disorder. This fear is described by clients as feelings of being startled and frightened all the time, often for unknown reasons. They may struggle with a constant terror of reexperiencing a past traumatic event, suffer nightmares and intrusive thoughts, or possibly have fear of moving forward in their lives. Survivors most often describe waiting for "something bad" to happen, suffering feelings of impending doom. Unwanted panic seems to come out of nowhere and can be embarrassing.

A perfect example of how post-traumatic stress rears its ugly head happened when my client Harry and his sister, Claudia, went into an ice-cream shop when he was about three years old and she was six. One of the waiters behind the counter, who just wanted to play with the children, picked Harry up and began swinging him around. But to Harry and his sister who had both been used to suffering sudden, physical beatings by an out-of-control, alcoholic father, this experience felt like just another unpredictable assault.

Claudia began screaming at the top of her lungs in fear that the waiter would hurt Harry. This brought the foster parents (not the original abusers) running into the ice-cream shop. The waiter explained to them that he was just kidding around, but the shock and fear of being "assaulted" by yet another adult and the fear that something terrible was going to happen permeated the rest of the children's afternoon, and it took much calming down before they could go into an ice-cream shop again.

In adulthood, Harry couldn't connect why he was always anxiety ridden as an older man with the trauma he experienced in childhood. His answer to any suggestion that one might be related to the other was, "Well, it's time for me to get over it, then." He was convinced his constant fear of the unknown was the reason for his escalated anxiety. He was surprised and somewhat relieved when he worked on the Affective Memory Exercise and recreated, through all his five senses, the ice-cream parlor and the whole event of being twirled around by the waiter.

Once the feeling from a memory surfaces, it is automatically transformed; it changes, and then, instead of it controlling you, you go on to control it forever. The experience of remembering frightening childhood events, many that are not even remembered clearly, can cause acute anxiety, which can, in turn, precipitate displacement of the memory onto other things, something as simple as fear of elevators. By using the Affective Memory Exercise for this kind of fear, Harry was able to console himself that he could use good strategies to keep himself safe in adulthood.

It's like looking at a picture on a wall over and over again. At first it can be very moving, but then as you keep looking at it, it becomes just a picture, the emotions dissipate. In the same way, remembering fear can evoke fear reactions, but as you use reality and the truth of the situation, your fear becomes less and less. Unexpressed trauma can turn into long-term post-traumatic stress disorder. But if traumas are spoken out, and the feelings associated with these memories are reexperienced and expressed in the here and now, you will be able to integrate them into your current personality. The anxiety connected with it will abate.

Guilt

Guilt is anger turned inward toward the self. It is one emotion that is regularly reported by abuse survivors. It usually appears at the developmental stage of about three years old, when a child gets involved with other children and finds pride in such things as learning games and building sand castles.

However, if the abuse occurs during this crucial phase of development, a child can grow up surrounded by shame and doubt. Guilt can be complicated, as

I mentioned above, if you remember that you inadvertently enjoyed or became excited by the abuse, especially sexual abuse. If physical abuse, such as spankings and beatings, become sexualized in a child's mind, that child can become even more confused and feel dirty.

In therapy, survivors usually discover that as children, they unconsciously wished to be as powerful as their abuser. Now, as adults, they may secretly harbor a desire to take control over the abuser by abusing others. A survivor who saw her perpetrator as a cruel, overpowering force may think that she needs to be equally cruel and overpowering in order to be stronger than the abuser—in order to be "safe" from him or her. Some survivors fear having children for fear they'll abuse them. For them, working through this fear becomes one of the most important goals of treatment.

Identity Problems

Often abuse survivors complain they have no sense of their "identity." They tend to feel that their "real" selves have been brutalized out of them. Sometimes they find themselves wanting to take on the life of another person, acting like that person, taking on the same likes and dislikes, and perhaps dressing like that person. My friend Katie was once utterly besieged by a coworker who took on her persona to such a degree that even sports events that were important to Katie became events that were of paramount importance to her coworker. The situation almost became one of harassment when the coworker suddenly and without any seeming reason took on the look and affect of Katie, right down to her jewelry and dresses.

When your identity is stolen away by an abuser making you believe you are worthless, you may find yourself trying to pattern yourself after people who look like what you wish you could be. At least it seems like *something*. Perhaps you feel that you have no idea who you are. It's like you look inside, and there's no one home. Perhaps you wonder, because you don't quite know, what you want and what you dislike, what you think or feel. When you feel you are empty, you set yourself up for labels, accepting how other people define you. If someone calls you cold or selfish or immature or unable to give, perhaps you don't dispute them. You might figure, if that's what they say you're like, then that must be what you are. Sometimes you blindly accept these common labels from others because you don't know yourself well enough to know if the accusations are true.

The whole process of "copying" others to fit in reminds me of the old movie studio routine of telling contract players how to look, whom to date, what music and dance they like, what their hobbies are, and what they can and can't do in their lives. Their press agents revealed to the world who these stars were so that fans could identify with them; the star had a strong identity. But in truth, the studio ran every single bit of their lives. For some it must have felt stifling; but for others there was a structure that probably felt safe.

Abuse survivors are usually in the process of trying to figure out who they are at all times. What is "acceptable"? What would be "right"? The question of "acceptable to whom?" doesn't even register. Many survivors take a negative stance and ask, "Why am I different?" and "How can I look like the mainstream?" But what is the mainstream? Who are all these people who apparently fit in when we don't? And how do they handle feelings of inadequacy and "not being enough"?

The Portrait Exercise is tailor-made to help survivors flesh out who they are and what they want in their lives. This exercise allows them to take action and differentiate themselves from others in an empowering way. They are able to see themselves the way they want to be and with what they hope to achieve.

Isolation

When the demands of everyday life become too great for abuse survivors, they often isolate themselves. Isolation becomes a hiding behavior, a place where profound emptiness may be experienced as safer than the inescapable pain from the lack of empathy of others. Sometimes isolating may be a way of feeling complete by adopting an attitude of superiority to disguise feelings of inferiority.

An abuse survivor may divide herself into pieces emotionally and end up expressing incongruent feelings, sporting a happy face when in fact she may be raging, showing anger to cover fear, and so on. Isolation is also a way of hiding who you really are so that others will not intrude to judge and possible reject or wound. However, isolating also spares the survivor risking the authenticity of a relationship.

There is an answer, and it is acting out physically what you want right now on a stage or in front of a therapist and group. As you act out, speak out, or demonstrate what you need, more ideas will emerge that will help you define and attain your goals.

The Building a Room Exercise helps you edge your way into working with other people, slowly and deliberately, through creating a space of your own where others are invited in. There you will find a better solution to overcoming loneliness, making a place where you won't have to isolate yourself to feel safe.

Jealousy

What about jealousy? Is it a big part of your life? Do you find that you are jealous of friends, family, or even of your children? Do you find yourself competing with others in a way that always seems to make you feel that you are "not enough"?

When I was in college, I remember a girl who told me she was exhausted by trying to compete with other people to be the best. She was constantly comparing and contrasting herself to them, and in her mind, she always came up short. She said she yearned for the day that she would wake up and "everything would be all right with the world."

Jealousy can make you feel "less than," feel that everybody else has more than you do. There is never a time when you can relax and enjoy what you've created or own.

One of the best exercises for jealousy is the Dying Exercise. In it, survivors can look back on their lives and see in a flash what they would do differently. Because they imagine that time is running out, they often (amazingly) find the exact answer to how they can get what they always wished for. It can be a very empowering and exacting exercise and can really help you look at what you think is important in your life.

Loneliness

Loneliness can be perceived in two ways. One is that survivors perceive everyone as angry at them, lashing out and potentially dangerous, so they feel they have to isolate (even though they will get lonely) in order to protect themselves. The second is a shyness, timidity, and feeling like a social outcast. Both types of loneliness come from the impossibility for the child-abuse survivor to express emotion honestly and straightforwardly and have these emotions recognized and respected.

Different kinds of abuse predict different kinds of loneliness in adulthood. My client Melanie had been sexually abused in childhood by an uncle and a grandfather. She felt lonely and embarrassed in a crowd, believing everyone knew what had happened to her. Her first response to others was to feel fear and then to wish that the person would just "leave me alone."

Actors can perform for thousands in a theater, yet be lonely in their personal lives. They may be afraid that others will ridicule them or reject their performances. Rosalind Russell, an old-time actress of the 40s and 50s, said that acting is like "being naked in front of many people and then turning around slowly."

One of the best exercises to help all forms of loneliness is the Shower Exercise, where performers can "feel" their bodies without actually touching their skin. The exercise actually encompasses using the air, wind, water, or sun to imaginarily "feel" these elements on your skin. You can use your imagination to recreate the experience of feeling water—as in a shower—or feeling sunshine on your body. That may be the first time you notice you can re-own your physical self.

Lying

For me, the most surprising aftereffect of all kinds of child abuse is lying. Abuse survivors have been lied to by perpetrators, so it might appear that they would go out of their way to be as honest as possible. But, to the contrary, the deception and secrecy of their abuse often is the reason that they want to be anything but themselves.

As a therapist, and before that, as an actress, I could never understand how someone who lied to me would then try to diffuse their embarrassment at being caught at the lie, by telling me yet *another* lie to cover up the first one. Sometimes they would say something like, "Well, that's not what I meant." One producer I met, George, asked me to put a good deal of money into a project he was planning on producing. His promises were never-ending. He promised me a finder's fee and introductions to all sorts of important people if I would just help him raise the sum he needed.

George's own father had been a famous producer in New York. Apparently, his father had told George he could never be the success his father was. In fact, the father went so far as to say, "You will never amount to anything." This verbal onslaught caused George to throw himself into achieving success. But, instead of having a direction to achieving this success, George apparently felt that all he had to do was *say* it and it would be *true*. The very act of verbalizing what he wanted or what he believed somehow was enough—it made it magically true for him for the time being. And when you are in a magical fantasy, you have a way of maintaining the hope that your life can magically change, too.

I didn't have the money to give him that day, but later I heard from friends that George was a gambler and no money given to him ever found its way to a film! Lucky for me that I was insolvent that month.

Sometimes it's hard for me to fathom the kinds of things people lie about. My client Dolores used to tell lies that were immediately obvious. But as she put it, "The lie was worth it just to see the look on your face, even if, in the next minute, you'd find out I was lying!" When I asked her what the thrill in that was, she told me, "Because for those two minutes I was important. I was somebody who knew something or had something valuable that the others wanted. I could be what I thought others wanted me to be."

But Dolores was troubled by her lying. It was the reason she sought therapy. She found that she lied even when it didn't matter, when the lie was no more important or exciting than the truth. She lied about where she attended school, where she went on vacation, and even about men she dated. She loved to tell people that she had dated famous actors. Some of this chicanery was so easy to see through that it caused her considerable embarrassment. But getting caught still didn't deter her. She admitted, "I was addicted to not telling the truth."

Lying is the survivor's way of trying to live up to some arbitrary ideal garnered from someone else. Murray Bowen (1988), a famous psychiatrist, termed it the "false self" or "pseudo-self." It's that part of you that desires to live up to someone else's view of who you should be in order to feel accepted in the world.

All the "internal acting" exercises can allow you to circumvent lying by making it "all right" to be honest with how you feel, the truth of what happened to you, and your ability to deal with real situations in an honest and sincere way.

Negativity

Feeling bad about yourself leads to negativity. Survivors of childhood abuse and trauma often find that being negative is one of the many ways they sabotage themselves. Sometimes negativity can feel like strength and superiority, so initially putting someone down might appear to provide a survivor with a modicum of control and self-esteem. Negativity offers the added illusion of making others think the negative judgment is the right one, simply because it's negative. We think, well, maybe the naysayer knows something the rest of us don't. It's a way for the abuse survivor to get the attention she craves.

In psychology, every behavior has a need attached to it. Feeling bad about yourself may be a clue that you need to be heard, appreciated, seen. Perhaps in childhood the only way to accomplish all that before you could talk, was to cry. As an adult, you find yourself crying easily in an effort to gain sympathy and help instead of talking. Crying gains attention for you in a dramatic way. It really underlines your sense of hopelessness and despair—again, *learned* helplessness. With many abuse survivors, the uncertainty of how the abuse took place, sometimes the inner questioning of whether it *did* take place, and the survivor's feelings of contributing to it, cause much depression, doubt, and tears.

Rejection

Survivors often keep their true feelings hidden inside, kept secret, so that no one can reject them. Or they reject themselves, like in a Woody Allen movie, before anyone else can reject them. Fear of rejection is always a paramount theme in abuse survivors' stories. The abusive act, whether emotional, verbal, physical, or sexual, was in itself rejecting.

I've had clients describe how they've been rejected for so many jobs, turned down for so many auditions, and deserted in so many relationships that they give up when new chances come around again, convinced that no matter what they do, it won't matter, because someone will abuse them anyway. They feel fated to lose out. Many survivors say they suspect that they have an unconscious need to set themselves up for these rejection scenarios so they won't be surprised when they fail. They will have almost expected it. But they don't know exactly how they do it. Their belief that whatever they do won't be enough can actually precipitate continuing to do what *will* set them up for failure. It becomes a self-fulfilling prophecy.

Your ability to create and complete an exercise will be a good way to begin your quest to set up a positive and action-oriented life. As you continue working on many exercises, you will find that the support and guidance you always wanted and needed from others will be part of this work. Doing the exercises will help motivate you to continue healing by reaching out and connecting with people.

Sexual Addiction

It has been quite recent, only within the past two decades or so, that compulsive sexual behaviors, or sexual acting out, has been described. Compulsively seeking out sexual experiences can be an addiction in much the same way gamblers seek out card games or heroine addicts look for drugs. It can also be an aftereffect of early child abuse. If the survivor's sexual desires are not gratified, they may feel impaired and become depressed. They think they must find a sexual outlet before they can go on with the rest of their life.

Being a sex addict means you cannot control your behavior. One actress I knew reported that every time her agent got her a reading for a part, she needed to have sex with someone. Many abuse survivors will try repeatedly to have sex with as many people as they can as a way of being totally absorbed in a pleasurable and immediately gratifying activity. This behavior is also a way of trying to take control over the sexual experience suffered as a child, and sometimes sex with many is used to make sure you never get too close to any one person.

Some survivors may veer away from any sexual contact. In therapy, they need to learn how to separate the idea of sexual abuse from the idea of sexual love. Too many sexually abused children grow up never wanting sex because they don't want to see their lover as their abuser, and having sex with anyone, even their lover, threatens to trigger these awful thoughts.

Because many child-abuse survivors don't want to feel anything (it's too painful), they actively suppress their emotions by telling themselves they simply don't have any. Clients have described romantic situations in which they were much more successful in bed with partners they did not care about. When they were in bed with people they did care for, they escaped by "numbing out." Some abuse survivors cling onto a fantasy of being "rescued." They want a prince to come along and gallop them off to safety and love. This fantasy often goes hand in hand with sexual acting out. The survivor tells himself or herself that they are not really promiscuous—they are merely looking for that special person who will finally keep them safe.

The Inner Monologue Exercise will help those who depend only on fantasy to live their lives. It will help you to express yourself inside to yourself—help you figure out what you really need when you act out sexually. The exercise is especially useful in helping you work out an important decision by yourself or bolstering your confidence in your ability to accomplish an important mission.

Splitting

Splitting is a well-studied phenomenon. It refers to survivors dividing every person or experience into being *all good* or *all bad*. There never seems to be any gray areas.

In therapy, survivors learn how splitting takes place. They discover how they split people and relationships in order to satisfy their need to create an idealized relationship. When Mother or Dad could not live up to the child's idealized vision, they suddenly plummeted from grace.

Only when a child realizes that Mom and Dad are human and make mistakes, and can accept their mistakes as human frailties, can he or she get the parents off the pedestal and have a more realistic vision of them. That is the moment of maturity for the child.

By acting out situations in which splitting may naturally occur, such as in a fight with your best friend, you will begin to differentiate between what is personal, professional, and what simply *is*. In many instances, survivors discover that splitting doesn't need to happen at all; they are able to tolerate another's quirks and recognize that another's personality is simply different from their own, not better, not worse—just different.

Marcus was the perfect example of someone who constantly split people into those who were his best friends and those who were his mortal enemies. He expected a lot from a friendship, and the first time anyone let him down or did not live up to his exalted view of who they should be, he dumped them, refusing to ever speak to them again. Of course, he soon found himself in a depression because he felt a lack of closeness and support in his life.

The Animal Exercise helped him investigate what he expected from others so that he could be fairer in his impressions of them. But there are many acting exercises that can help survivors close the split by understanding how another person thinks so they can see that their own personality is not inexorably linked with anyone else's. Survivors *do* have individual personalities that stand apart from others.

Stealing

Amelia, the student I talked about earlier in the section on cheating, segued from cheating on tests in her teens to stealing from department stores in her twenties. She enjoyed using her wiles to devise new ways of pilfering clothes without being caught. At one point, someone not realizing she was carrying merchandise illegally out of the store actually held the door open for her!

Because she had never experienced the feeling of "buy it—you like it." She never experienced the freedom to buy something regardless of its price. She was always compelled to make sure that whatever she wanted to buy was not only affordable, but that it was absolutely necessary to own. As a child, her parents made her feel that if she didn't need it right now and bought it anyway, she was being frivolous and wasteful. Her constant calculations of whether or not she really should buy something contributed to a sense of having to be a perfectionist in adulthood. She had no freedom and was never able to allow herself to have fun.

Amelia finally "exploded one day" and took fifteen cookbooks out of a department store. She couldn't believe how easy it was, which just encouraged her to steal more. When she finally came to therapy, she had stolen over $100,000 worth of merchandise. She eventually got too scared to continue her thievery after seeing a story on television about a shoplifter who got a prison sentence after a successful two-year shoplifting run. Amelia was afraid her own luck was about to run out.

In therapy, I had Amelia use the Sensory Object Exercise to get her to visualize all the things she had ever wanted but had never been able to get in childhood. In her middle class family, even though her father had been an accountant and her mother a nurse, she was made to feel that she had to account for every penny she spent. But she was also told by her parents that she had to be friends with the girls in school who owned things. They told her "it's just as easy to have rich friends as poor ones." This paradoxical message was impossible to manage. Her would-be friends purchased expensive clothes and were able to eat out or go to movies or the mall on a regular basis. In fact, Amelia never had the feeling of plenty in her home, and yet she was expected to be grateful that her parents gave her food, shelter, and clothing. That was enough.

Stealing and getting away with it allowed Amelia to lose her feelings of impoverishment—after all, she felt she could have whatever she wanted by just taking it. The very act of taking something that didn't belong to her was payback for being cheated out of a childhood and for never having the right clothing to be accepted by her schoolmates.

Entitlement is often an aftereffect of childhood abuse, and stealing, rather than speaking out, is a way survivors can express their neediness when they have no voice to call out for help. Often they report that they were not allowed to need something as a child, or they were afraid of hurting a parent's feelings by asking for what they needed.

During acting exercises and in the safety of the therapeutic setting, survivors begin to uncover the "why" of stealing. There they can begin to allow themselves to symbolically restore what was emotionally stolen from them—their basic human need to be heard and respected.

Substance Abuse

If you have problems with drinking, gambling, sex, or smoking, you are already "acting out." Addictions are usually used to create a *persona,* a false self.

Think about how you have used your addictions to unleash your freedom to create, to be real. If you are recovering from any of these addictions, you know that you are now able to activate your imagination without them. In the case of smoking, as bad a habit as it is, it was probably originally there for you to relax, put an end to a day, or feel confident in a conversation—a tool used to help you deal with your life, perhaps to help you overcome embarrassment, humiliation, or shame.

You probably discovered that you were able to create those same calm feelings without a cigarette or a drink once you made the commitment to stop the addiction. In fact, you were even better able to express yourself and be creative than when you had been under the influence of a substance.

Addictions of all kinds may feel like an interim way of discovering your *true self.* Drinking alcohol and using drugs to aid in disinhibition causes many abuse survivors to think they have a voice *only* when they are using substances. The drug becomes a "pal" because it seems to allow the survivor to feel free of embarrassment.

Addictions can also be used for self-medication against the pain of remembering abuse. That's why using imagination and creating or recreating moments in your life through acting exercises can work positively rather than negatively for you.

Instead of addictions and other harmful ways of trying to medicate the effects of abuse, acting exercises offer a positive, action-oriented, and healthy approach to reaching better results: like remembering the abuse and integrating the feelings surrounding it without punishing your body with drugs and alcohol.

Trust Problems

Basic trust, learned in infancy, is critical to human development. It's the most basic function we possess. It goes back to the cave. It is our "intuition," our "animal instinct." It is what we need for our very survival.

Trusting yourself means that you are able to size up a person or situation and tell what's true and real and what isn't. A good rule of thumb is, *If you feel it in your gut, you're probably right.*

The inability to trust is one of the most devastating aftereffects of childhood abuse. Learning to trust is the foundation for becoming a successful person in life, and a lack of trust is the foundation for developing a load of dysfunctional behaviors. When you cannot even trust your own judgment and intuition, you have a foundation built on sand.

In infancy, a child's trust in parents or primary caregivers is supposed to develop during the very first year of life. If a child has abusive experiences and learns not to trust the people closest to him, how can he ever trust anyone else?

Working through trust issues in conventional therapy can take years, but insights into how you lack trust can be uncovered by using some of the exercises in this book with some of your current life experiences. Exercises such as the Preparation-Before-a-Scene can actually help you get the nerve to risk going out with someone new. A wonderful exercise called the Academy Award will help you uncover secret desires and help you reveal to yourself the way you can attain them. Through these acting exercises, abuse survivors (as well as actors) can begin to acquire self-trust. As you amass more confidence, you will strengthen your ability to trust in others—first in the "audience" of a group or individual therapy session, and ultimately in your personal relationships.

Too Nice

Have you ever forgiven someone too soon for an injury they did to you or a transgression that hurt you? Are you the one who is always ready to say, "It's okay," even when you know that the other person is being selfish and is taking advantage of you—and will do it again?

Doing too much for someone you hardly know or care about—being "too nice"—can be another telltale symptom of childhood abuse. It springs out of shame and low self-esteem.

My teaching assistant at college, Barry, was always doing students' homework for them. He never flunked anyone, and he tirelessly tutored people by giving them answers to exam questions. He even did jobs for other teaching assistants that were not his to do, and he spent lots of his own money to pay bills for those less fortunate. Whenever a friend needed a helping hand, Barry was the first one on site

But instead of getting the thanks that he felt he deserved for his seeming selflessness, Barry was criticized and demeaned, even made fun of. He was just too nice. It was hard for others (and rightly so) to trust his motives. As one student complained, "He has such a compulsion to do things for me that it makes me suspect it's not really for me."

In therapy, Barry did the Preparation Before a Scene exercise and discovered that his over-the-top working for others was so intense that even he would have had a hard time trusting someone like himself! He realized that underneath the surface (he was agreeable to a fault) and underneath all those seemingly nice actions, he was swimming in low-self esteem and seething with rage over his wife's infidelity. She'd had a string of affairs, and he'd pretended not to notice. By doing for others, Barry tried to prop up his sagging self-esteem and was able to tell himself he was a nice guy, superior to those men his wife dated, and therefore didn't deserve to be betrayed.

But being too nice is really a manipulation. Survivors can tell themselves that because they are doing good deeds, it means they are really good people. It allows them to sidestep feeling guilty, probably for what they assume they must have done to bring about the abuse situation. By trying to make everybody like you, or trying to correct every wrong, a survivor feels he or she is correcting or undoing the wrongs from the past that were done to him.

How Change Begins

Well, after all that, you may wonder how change begins? Keep in mind, if you found yourself in the list of symptoms above and have decided that you, too, are being held back in life by some of these aftereffects (even if you cannot remember or didn't experience child abuse), then it's time to do something about it, time to uncover what's behind the symptoms and begin to heal them. Then and only then can you begin to find ways of improving what Freud called the two most important areas in life: love and work.

It's time now to discover a way to stop avoiding intimacy, playing it safe, avoiding risk, or compulsively attaching yourself to sex, alcohol, drugs, gambling, work, or other escapes. You can now begin to have more satisfaction in your work, be more successful and secure financially, and have winning relationships. That way is with acting exercises. You are about to embark on a fascinating journey where you will peel off layers of feelings so that your old traumas will no longer continue to haunt you and trip you up. Wouldn't it be nice to be in control of your personal life? Do you think success would scare you? What do you imagine success feels like inside? Warm and satisfying? Or scary and demanding?

Acting exercises can help you find out.

Part Two

External Acting Exercises and How They Work

Chapter 3

The Exercises: External to Internal

The Onion

From the beginning of their development our emotions are layered, like a huge onion. Each assault to our feelings is covered over by the next feeling to protect us from unbearable hurt. These cover-ups, so to speak, happen unconsciously. You might remember how you used to escape from emotional pain as a child. Perhaps you hid in a special place, lost yourself in reading books, or had a special friend at whose house you escaped the frenzy and fear you experienced at your home. We tend to "forget" some of the bad things that happened by pushing them deep into the unconscious where it's hard to get to them. But these feelings fester there and come back to us as dysfunctional actions in adulthood.

As you begin to work on these acting exercises, you will notice the hierarchy that guides exercising. Each exercise will enable you to peel off another layer of pain to expose the feelings you have unconsciously hidden underneath. All of the memories and experiences that may seem far away (but that actually come back and visit you unexpectedly) will be uncovered and dealt with in a mature way. The beauty of working this way is to enable you to gain control over exactly how much you want to remember, feel, or experience without your becoming overwhelmed or frightened.

Object relations therapy is an uncovering therapy where the hope is that you will be able to make your unconscious mind conscious. Remember, according to Freud (1938), the mind has three levels: the conscious or highest level, where you are aware that you are thinking, feeling, and processing; the subconscious mind, which is just underneath the conscious and where you know things, but cannot actually recall them immediately; and the unconscious mind where only feelings reside.

Even though this is an uncovering process, memories can pop up from the unconscious at any time.

Acting exercises are done in two stages: First you'll do the external acting exercises to help you to create objects that can be anything you usually deal with in your world. As I said earlier, a coffee or tea cup that you either use every day or an imaginary one which comes to mind will serve as the first example to you that you can remember and remember well. Since you will not be using a real, material cup, but will be creating one from memory, you will also see how your unconscious works. Here you will be using texture and touch to recreate. As you put your arm out in front of you, the palm of your hand turned upward, you will look into your hand and a cup of some kind will appear. That cup will have meaning for you, and it's the meaning and feeling that we are after.

Second, you'll do the internal acting exercises, during which abuse survivors experience their internal world through their five senses of sight, sound, touch, smell, and taste. Memories of people and events begin to come forward through this indirect beckoning of sense memories. In this way, survivors are able to create and explore atmosphere, which is your surroundings, but not necessarily environments in your real world. I've had clients who put themselves on the moon to find solace and peace.

The External Acting Exercises

- The Coffee Cup Exercise
- The Shower Exercise
- The Fourth Wall Exercise
- The Atmosphere Exercise
- The Building a Room Exercise
- The Entrance and Exit Exercise
- The Mountain Exercise

The Internal Acting Exercises

- The Sense-Memory Exercise
- The Portrait Exercise
- The History Exercise
- The "As If" Exercise
- The Private Moment Exercise
- The Animal Exercise
- The Gibberish Exercise

- The Telephone Exercise
- The Academy Award Speech Exercise
- The Inner Monologue Exercise
- The Dying Exercise
- The Affective Memory Exercise
- The Preparation-Before-a-Scene Exercise

Combining Exercises

Once all the external and internal exercises have been successfully completed, you can then begin to combine them. Sometimes two external exercises can be combined, at others times two internal exercises work well together. Then we can combine an external with an internal exercise to get a complete sense of your experience.

The second to last internal exercise is called the Affective Memory Exercise. Here, all objects, feelings, and memories from your past abuse come to the fore. And, because you will have successfully completed the earlier exercises, you will feel free to safely reexperience your abuse situation. The difference in experiencing them in the here and now is that you are now an adult with adult feelings and insight and more power and control. The last exercise, "Preparation-Before-a-Scene," will allow you to finally use all the previous exercises in order to confront your abuser for real, or in your head.

First Things First—The Sunshine Exercise (A Relaxation Technique)

I noticed, both as an acting coach and later as a licensed psychotherapist, that my students/clients not only needed to feel safe in their environments before they could risk anything emotional, but they also needed to feel comfortable internally. The best way of reaching this state, I found, is to begin with a relaxation exercise.

All the exercises that follow in this book begin with a good relaxation exercise. Actors with formal training almost universally use this exercise before doing their work or doing any of the other exercises. The reason for this is simple: Your concentration and ability to create are impaired if you are nervous, jumpy, or unable to focus on what you're doing. Actors try to empty their minds of all extraneous thoughts before they rehearse. In therapy, the same thing helps.

Even though the Sunshine Exercise that follows is one that is used in a multitude of therapies, as well as in acting situations, you can do it alone. It starts with relaxing all the muscles in your body and clearing your mind of outside stimuli. It does take time, especially in the beginning, to turn off the brain chatter so that you can get into the exercise and focus your attention on the task at hand.

Do not begin this exercise if you are in a rush, or if you cannot spend at least fifteen minutes on it—especially the first few times you do it.

What Relaxation Means

Relaxation means that you are going to begin to trust yourself enough to put yourself in charge of your thoughts and emotions. For survivors, this can be scary. It also means that you must become aware of how and where tension accumulates in your body.

Now let's take a look at how you can expand your ability to trust in yourself immediately. You are going to begin to relax each part of your body individually. When I work on this exercise with a new client, I usually ask that person to open his or her eyes occasionally to pinpoint where I am in the room in order to help them feel secure. This also enhances their control over how much or how little they wish to do. For abuse survivors, there is no need to add to the post-traumatic stress of surprise, so I often invite my clients simply to keep their eyes opened.

The Sunshine Exercise (The Ultimate Relaxation Exercise)

1. Find a comfortable yet firm chair, one where you can slouch and feel secure, but not one so comfortable that you'll fall asleep.

2. Get into a relaxed, unencumbered position in that chair.

3. Close your eyes (if you wish) and let your head fall wherever it may. Just make sure your head feels supported so that you can concentrate on the exercise and not get a crick in your neck. You may let your arms fall naturally at your sides; spread your legs slightly apart for support, then just let the chair hold you.

4. Depending on how relaxed you feel, you might open your eyes for a short time to center yourself, then close them and continue to relax your body. Again, the point is for you to begin to experience control over your body.

5. Start by using any one of a number of images. A favorite in my acting class is to imagine yourself at the beach and allow the sun to warm your body. You can easily create your own relaxation exercise with music, calling on each of your muscle groups to relax, or by using the image of waves to encompass and calm your body from your feet to the top of your head. Many people use water images, but sexual abuse survivors may not feel as comfortable using this image. Most people like to feel warm, so initially you can imagine you are on a beautiful beach in the Caribbean or just lying in your backyard.

6. Begin by imagining the sun on your entire body at first. Ask yourself specific questions such as "Where is the warmth most intense, on my stomach or thighs? On my arms?"

7. Now begin to focus your mind on the particular muscle groups in your body. Take them one at a time. For instance, you might begin with your toes. Just let your mind think about them and how they feel right now.

8. Now begin to concentrate just on your left foot. If you have chosen a sun image, then slowly feel the warmth of the sun touching each toe, the top of your foot, and the heel of your foot. Really feel where the heat is most intense and where your foot is barely warm.

9. Next, focus on your right foot. Again, feel where the sun is first hitting it. Be specific and detailed. Imagine sunlight warming each of your toes. Take your time.

10. Once you feel that you have gained as much as you can from your concentration on your feet, slowly begin to feel the warmth move up your legs from your ankles to your knees. Stop at your knees. Where can you especially feel the heat of the sun on your legs? Does the heat you feel on the top of your legs differ from the heat on the back of your legs, away from the sunlight?

11. Now consider the thigh area. Allow the heat to come up your legs and onto your thighs. Feel its warmth on both thighs and then move it up to your lower stomach. Feel where the heat is most intense on your stomach. Where is it cooler? Never use the relaxation exercise on your sexual areas. We want to concentrate simply on groups of muscles that will relax you. Slowly move the sun onto the lower part of your abdomen, near your belly button. See if you can feel its warmth across the lower part of your stomach.

12. Then, slowly, let the sun begin to warm your chest, begin to warm your shoulders, then your arms.

13. Now imagine the sunshine warming both your arms, from your shoulders first, down to your elbows, and then from your elbows down your lower arms to your wrists. If you like, you can concentrate on one arm at a time. For instance, focus on the sun's warmth going down the left arm first to the elbow. From the elbow to the wrist. Then allow the sun to warm your hand and each of your fingers in turn. Then the right arm to the elbow and onto the forearm, hand, and fingers. Try to notice whether it feels different where certain areas of your body are in direct sunlight and other parts aren't. Is it cooler in areas hidden from the sun?

14. Lastly, allow the sun to warm your face. Notice how the muscles relax and how smooth your skin feels. As you feel your body relax, bask in the warmth and keep testing each muscle group to make sure it is truly relaxed.

The Sunshine Exercise is the first exercise any actor will learn in order to prevent tension, which cause actors to revert to "actor tricks" to contain their insecurity or feelings of not knowing what they are doing truthfully in the part. You have undoubtedly seen some of these actor affectations that have nothing to do with the character or the way the character might behave. These tricks can be: the actor saying lines too loudly, rubbing the outside of one arm, or the actor trying to show emotion when he or she doesn't really feel it by grimacing or biting the lip as they say a line to show they are about to cry. Actors casting their eyes down to display worry is another favorite. You can see these tricks in any actor who's not sure whether or not he or she has captured the character and needs to make sure you, the audience, get what they're trying to do.

Often, before becoming aware of how the Sunshine Exercise can help, these "acting aids" are all an actor has to depend on to stem feeling not real as the character. But any amount of fear will prevent creation, so fear must be contained in a good relaxation exercise.

The Sunshine Exercise is also the one exercise that allows actors to have a clean slate to prepare themselves for the next exercise or for the next scene they play. But for the rest of us, relaxation allows our priorities to come forward in an unhurried, natural way. Once you have mastered the exercise, you will be ready to begin the other exercises. But don't rush through it. It does take time to master.

I always enjoyed watching actors do this exercise in front of my acting coach, Lee Strasberg. Four or five acting students would sit on the stage at once, and Lee would walk among them, picking up an arm or a leg here and there to test for relaxation. Presumably, if an actor had truly relaxed his or her body, Strasberg would be able to pick up the arm or leg and let it drop where it may. However, if a person were still tense, when Lee picked up the limb, that actor would invariably help him by lifting their arm for him, thus proving that they were not at all relaxed.

But many students were very fearful and submissive in front of such a famous coach, and after about five minutes—when the actor looked like they were so relaxed they could go to sleep—Lee would begin his walk to test their relaxation. There was always one unfortunate actor who would nearly jump out of the chair the minute Strasberg touched them: He or she was so scared at being "tested" by the great coach that they found it almost impossible to relax. The class would laugh, and the poor actor would have to start trying to relax all over again.

What I noticed, however, was that once an acting student had been in class for a period of time, his or her trust would begin to build up enough to allow their relaxation abilities to become a little more secure.

Remember, this exercise is just like anything else you try in life—the first time is the hardest. The more you do the exercise, the less time it will take you to become entirely relaxed. After about fifteen minutes, you will notice your body becoming truly pliable and calm. That's when acting is most honest and survivors find their voices. While doing the exercise, ask yourself positive, action-oriented questions, such as:

- Where is my neck tense?
- Where is my back feeling relaxed?
- Are my leg and arm muscles relaxed?
- Where am I not relaxed?

These questions will help you concentrate, and they will also evoke feelings. The first thing you might notice are the places in your body where fear, anxiety, and tenseness pool themselves. Be aware of just *where* in your body your emotions are particularly apparent. Some people feel fear in their stomach and chest areas; others notice their hands shaking. Just note that the anxiety is there; you will discover that it dissipates as you relax other parts of your body.

Now begin to think about the first thing that comes into your mind as you sit, relaxed. Whatever pops up unexpectedly, whether it is a memory of what happened yesterday or plans of what you need to do today, will be the most important thing on your mind right now. Remember, unexpected thoughts are your unconscious mind speaking to you and letting you know where you are in your life today. We are going to use those thoughts and emotions in a positive way to help you relax. For example, if your first thought is, "I've got to pay that Visa bill," you've just prioritized what you need to do before you can begin to feel calm and relaxed. Acknowledge that you will pay the bill and repeat in your mind, "Empty your mind, empty your mind."

If you thought, "This exercise is really silly," it may be the first indication you have that you feel uncomfortable, a feeling that doing things in front of others embarrasses you or compromises the sense of self that you have built up to protect yourself. Perhaps this type of thought process allows you to hide your real self.

Hierarchy

Please keep in mind that these exercises are done best in a hierarchical manner so that little by little, memories, feelings, and recollections can emerge or unfold. As you will see in the Coffee Cup Exercise, your imagination is really at your fingertips as you recreate the object.

As you continue to use your body and your mind together in creating each exercise, you may notice that each exercise opens you up to these feelings more and more. As information and feelings surface, you may also notice that your past abuse and perhaps current abuses become clearer in your mind.

Just like the professional actor in a role, you will be involved in a progressive revelation of feelings and memories, and you will be putting yourself in control of how much or how little you wish to feel at any given time. So if something begins to feel overwhelming, stop whatever you are doing and go back to the previous exercise; or better still, do the relaxation exercise again until your comfort level increases. As you use each exercise to uncover the feelings of abuse, slowly and privately and at your own pace, you will find it easier to begin opening up to others and voicing your experiences. Then you will be able to take control over the shame, guilt, and humiliation resulting from these discoveries.

The Third Eye

After the Sunshine (Relaxation) Exercise has been mastered, I usually ask clients to consider the "third eye" phenomenon to keep feeling safe inside. The third eye is that part of you that always knows exactly where you are and what you are doing as you go through all this. At any given moment in an exercise, you can stop, get up from the chair or leave the stage, and announce to yourself or to others, "I've had enough—too much stuff is coming up for me to handle." Actors always do that. If you find yourself becoming overwhelmed by a remembrance, you will stop whatever you're doing and go back to the previous exercise, or better still, to the relaxation exercise until your comfort level increases.

So, please note: If you worry that you'll get yourself into a scary mental state from which it will be hard to escape, use your third eye. The third eye is a constant reminder that you are in control. If you are still panicked about working alone in your imagination, invite a friend to participate with you as an observer when you first begin the exercises. If you are currently in therapy, ask your therapist if you can try some of these exercises during a regular session.

The Fear Pool

We've all heard the phrase, "I'm too scared to try anything new," or, "It's too late—I'm already who I am." You may recognize these sentiments as fear, pure and simple. Fear *pools* itself in certain situations or affiliations; for example, speaking in public is one of them. But these fear pools are just what you want to uncover in order to integrate them into your personality, take control of them, and set yourself free of them. Once you begin to change your life, you increase your knowledge of how powerful you really are in your life. That's how the exercises will work for you.

Okay, Ready to Roll

Remember what we are looking for in doing these exercises: memories and the feelings that come up from them. Now that you know the theory behind the exercises, let's deal with the reality. The first exercise involves imagining something simple that is available to you in everyday life—a cup. The Coffee Cup Exercise is the first "object"exercise, where survivors will begin their journey into their imaginations where they will create an imaginary object, and have control over what they will create. Here's where you can make positive things happen in your life and you can push out negative ones.

Chapter 4

The Coffee Cup Exercise

How External Exercises Work

The external acting exercises were originally designed to help actors create, explore, and experience their make-believe environments on the stage. However, for abuse survivors, these exercises act as a safe beginning to abandon a seemingly safe fantasy life and begin to explore their outward reality. These exercises will help you create your environment so that you can explore your feelings in it.

In these exercises, you will be using objects from both your past and present to bring up specific feelings. As each object is realized, you will be enhancing your ability to create whatever you want from your imagination. That can begin to help you feel mentally strong. This may be the first time you have ever experienced empowerment or taken the first steps toward better self-esteem and a positive self-image. The external exercises will allow you, a trauma or abuse survivor, to safely delve deeper and deeper into your unconscious mind.

As each exercise feels complete, you will be more likely to attempt the next one, and so on, until you are able to do all the exercises completely and fully. The more adept you become, the more easily you will be able to use two or three of these exercises at once to create a real scene from your life.

The external exercises help you integrate your feelings with your environment. Memories will emerge that allow you to link your current feelings with past emotions. That will help you gain insight into how you created old patterns, which are now infiltrating your current behavior.

Remember, too, to do the relaxation exercise first. You need to be fully relaxed. Without good relaxation, we tend to anticipate the next thing we need to do, worry over whether or not we are doing the exercises correctly, or worry about whether or not all this will really help. Once you have trained yourself to relax, you will find that experiences and feelings will come to you easily just by thinking about them.

Lastly, as you finish each external acting exercise, either write down or tape record your feelings that come up from the exercise. If an exercise feels too threatening or overwhelming, stop it immediately, go back to the relaxation exercise, and ask yourself, "What do I want to create?"

Remember: These exercises have a hierarchical rationale, so **do them in order.**

The Coffee Cup Exercise

The Coffee Cup Exercise is the first exercise where you will begin to create your external environment in order to help your mind and your body remember the past. The very fact that you *can* create something imaginary will act as proof that you can take back the power of your mind. It is the first onion layer to begin to peel off to help you look at a memory or a feeling that might be just below the surface of your consciousness

1. Extend your arm in front of you as far as you can right now; open your hand with your palm facing up. Now, allow you imagination to put a coffee (or tea) cup in that palm. See how it just automatically appears in imagination to you? You probably didn't have to do anything other than *will* it there. Obviously, you can't actually see the cup, but it is there in your mind's eye.

2. Now, with your other hand, begin to "touch" the cup. *Speaking out loud,* describe the cup sensorially. That is, what do you "feel" its size and shape are? Instead of saying, "This is a large cup with a thick, ceramic handle," use words that only describe your five senses of touch, taste, smell, sight, or sound. For example, to use the sense of touch, you might say, "This part of the cup feels cold," then feel another part of the cup, "This is the part that feels warm."

3. To use your sense of taste, put the cup to your lips and take a "sip" from it. Can you "taste" the coffee? What is the temperature of the liquid inside: hot or cold? Does it taste piquant, sweet, sour, or bitter? Can you imagine the real taste of coffee, tea, Postum, chocolate, or whatever else you have put in the cup?

4. To use your sense of smell, simply put your nose to the rim of your imaginary cup and take a deep breath. Remember what coffee smells like? Can you smell it?

5. "Look" at your cup. Use your sense of sight by saying, "The cup is big (or small), it is the color of (whatever color your cup is), and it is shaped like (whatever shape you image the cup to be).

6. And finally, use your sense of sound by "pinging" the imaginary cup to see if it resonates with a thud or a clear, crystal sound—perhaps of fine china.

7. Now, keeping the cup in one hand, use the other hand to investigate the texture of the cup by rubbing your hand around the rim. Does it feel bumpy or smooth? Is it porcelain or some other material? Is that texture sharp or dull? Does the material of the cup remind you of a person, place, holiday, or special occasion? What about the body of the cup? Is it fat and round, tall and thin, or an odd shape? How does the cup feel in your hand? Really try to feel its weight. Does it fit into your palm, or is it a big mug that is tipsy in your grasp? Try to lift the cup up and feel its heaviness or lightness. Do you find that you are really getting the sense of your cup?

   Remember, keep talking out loud. Ask yourself leading questions about your cup to further enhance your belief in it. What kind of cup is this? Is it a cup that the czars of Russia might have drunk from, or is it a common mug from a coffee house? Here, you might notice how differently you will handle your cup depending on your answer to that question. If this is a cup a czar might drink from, you're probably likely to hold it carefully, concerned about dropping it. If it is from a coffee house, you probably handle it less carefully, less cautiously.

8. Now ask yourself, "When did I get this cup?" What do you remember about the circumstances or the story surrounding receiving the cup? Did you buy it for yourself, or was it a gift from someone special? Is this a real or imaginary memory? Is your cup a fantasy that you just created for the sake of the exercise? Or is it a cup you would like to buy someday? What do you think made your unconscious think of this particular cup today?

9. Increase your concentration now by continuing to speak out loud. Keep speaking in terms of sight, sound, touch, smell, and taste.

   Remember, the sensory apparatus in your body holds all your secret memories and feelings about everything that has ever happened to you. It will allow you to remember the past much more clearly and readily than if you became "cerebral" and just tried to recount your memories intellectually.

10. So keep framing your questions with positive, active verbs such as "What am I smelling now?" If you speak out about the past or what usually happens, you will be intellectually (instead of sensorially) creating your objects. So instead of saying something like, "Usually when I smell coffee it makes me sick to my stomach," you might say, "This smell is strong, hot, and cinnamon-like." See the difference? Keep your questions and answers in the present tense and action oriented: "I am now smelling, or seeing etc. . . ."

Clara's Cup

Clara was a twenty-seven-year-old woman whose husband of two years came home from the office one night and asked for a divorce. Clara was stunned, but she couldn't feel anything. She couldn't cry or even understand what had happened. Their sex life was active, they had friends together, and Clara was even considering having a baby. But her husband wanted her to move out of their house immediately. He gave no explanation, so Clara refused to leave.

Instead, for another year she stayed in the house and locked herself in a tiny maid's quarters while her husband lived in their bedroom and entertained a number of girlfriends. Clara said nothing and remained fearful that he might at anytime become violent. Finally, her husband moved out and Clara was left wondering what had happened.

But despite all that abuse, it still took another five years for Clara to finally agree to a divorce. In therapy, she couldn't connect with what was keeping her in the prison of her home. She remembered her mother, who was always frightened. But her memories were vague, and she felt they held little meaning for her now. Clara simply couldn't *feel* how hurt and humiliated she had been all her life. All she felt was her own guilt at not being successful in her marriage. Hours in therapy were spent speculating how she could get her marriage back or manipulate her husband into being the person she needed him to be.

As with Lisa, the Coffee Cup Exercise was a breakthrough for Clara. The cup that appeared in her opened palm was a baby cup, one of those silver, tiny mugs that are often given at baby showers. And to her surprise, there on the side of the cup, engraved in silver, was Clara's name. Memories flooded into her mind. Things she had never been able to talk about before suddenly could no longer be held back. She remembered her mother, a prostitute who had contracted Huntington's chorea, a fatal illness that usually kills people in middle age. Before her illness, her mother had slept with a "john" one night and became pregnant with Clara. The problem was, there was no place for a child in her mother's life.

Her father disappeared after that encounter, and Clara's mother began taking the child with her on "dates." She was dragged from one location to another throughout East Los Angeles, once even hit by a car so that she had to spend the night at the county hospital. She was often left to fend for herself in an alley during early morning hours while her mother was "busy." Clara bore physical as well as mental scars from these ordeals.

When Clara was nine her mother died, and the mother's friends, other prostitutes, literally took over the child's care. She found herself a child in a "house" of prostitution. The girls were kind to her, but some of their "dates" weren't. Some johns wanted the nine-year-old sexually. At one point she had been raped by a customer in the house, and another time she had been severely beaten by a john for watching him with one of the girl's. But on Clara's tenth birthday, the "madam" of the house saw a cup in a pawnshop with the name "Clara" already etched on it and bought it for the child. It was the happiest memory of Clara's life.

In therapy, she discovered that the negative thoughts that filled her unconscious mind were variations of, "If I'm not good, people I love will be taken away from me. I need to be perfect." From the moment of that discovery, the sense of abandonment and the fear of depending on others who were not safe became the focus of Clara's therapy.

The Coffee Cup Exercise enabled Clara to connect with her constant fear of loss. What was the truth, the reality of her situation? The cup had brought her back emotionally to a time in her life when she was first aware of how unsteady and insecure she felt with her caretakers. It also enabled her to take a look at why she had stayed in her abusive, constricting marriage: She had been afraid of being left all alone again with no money, no love, and no prospects for ever having these things. In therapy, she began to connect with how she felt as a child: being at the mercy of more powerful people who would surely abuse her and abandon her. Where was her strength? she wondered.

As she continued on to the Shower Exercise, more memories emerged of the way strangers had ridiculed her prepubescent body. She began to recreate the panic she had always experienced when she had been left alone with a john. She could recall her early adversion to having children because she was not sure how she could protect them from suffering similar assaults from strangers. After all, she reasoned, she hadn't been able to protect herself. As she began the differentiation from her childhood experiences and began to relate to herself and her body as an adult, she began to find empowerment.

As we processed the terrible fate she envisioned for herself, she began to look at the truth of her life *right now*. She actually had money, the prospects of a good job were always there, she had many talents, and she had friends who were supportive. As she worked on rediscovering herself, she found the strength to call a friend with whom she worked at a power facility. She stayed for a short time with this friend while she found an affordable apartment for herself. She was finally able to move out of the house she had shared with her husband. Then she called Legal Aid and was given good information about where she could receive guidance about selling her home. With help from that agency, she divorced her husband and began to set up a life where she was in control. A few years later, she married a man who at first seemed *too nice*, and she again contemplated the possibility of divorce. He didn't "turn her on." But as she began to get comfortable with allowing herself to be nurtured, she realized she loved this person in a way she had never loved anyone. Once ashamed of her body, she began wearing clothes that showed off her figure, and her confidence was heightened even further.

Today, Clara lives with her husband of ten years in a beautiful area of Los Angeles with two children and a thriving career in show business. The Coffee Cup exercise was only the beginning of Clara's journey into her unconscious mind, the tip of the iceberg. Each step was exciting and even thrilling as she rediscovered the woman she was always *meant* to be before abuse entered the picture.

Now let's move on to some of the other equally powerful acting exercises. Next up is the Shower Exercise.

Chapter 5

The Shower Exercise

Beginning to Trust Your Body

The next stage in the exercise hierarchy comes with the Shower Exercise. In this exercise, your ability to begin to get in touch with your body and feel comfortable with it are explored. Feelings and memories of trauma and abuse may surface, but more likely, you will discover that your body belongs to you. By reading this book and doing the exercises you are beginning to make free choices. These sorts of choices are the basis for autonomy, you're ability to begin to take care of yourself in the world. Self-esteem and self-control depend on the confidence and pride you feel in your body. Doubt and shame come from fear of self-control—the constant fear mom or dad will chastise you every chance they get.

The Shower Exercise

The Shower Exercise involves paying attention to your body, your *whole* body. It also utilizes your sense of touch. For many survivors, touch has always been unpleasant, suggestive, or hurtful. With the Shower Exercise, you can begin to feel your own body without actually touching it. Your hands never really contact your skin. Instead, always keep your touch about one-half inch above your skin, so that you can work in your imagination. The idea is for emotions to emerge regarding how you feel about your body now. If you are uncomfortable imagining yourself nude in a shower, picture yourself showering fully dressed.

1. Do the Sunshine Exercise (the Relaxation Exercise) first.

2. Begin the Shower Exercise by imagining yourself standing in a shower.

3. What does the shower look like from the inside? Is it porcelain or tile? Is it encompassed in a bathtub combination? Is the showerhead spigot large or small? Is the shower door beveled glass or does a curtain hide a shower/tub combination? If it is a curtain, what color is it?

4. Now turn the water on. Does the water flow fast or slow, hot or cold as it comes out of the faucet? Do you know how to turn your particular shower on so that the water is exactly the right temperature? Or are you like most people, who experience the shower as either too hot or too cold at first? You might even feel like getting more creative and imagining that the showerhead has multiple settings in which water can flow on your body, making a pounding sensation, or released with a stronger flow and in a very specific direction.

5. Begin to feel the water on your body. Where does it hit first? How does it feel on different parts of your body? Note any sensations that come up for you. Sounds a bit like *Psycho*? Well, for you it's just an exercise.

6. Feel specific parts of your body in the shower. Again, do *not* actually touch your skin. Instead, keep your "feel" just about an inch away from your actual flesh so that your senses can work in imagination. That is how you control how much or how little you wish to do.

7. If you have chosen to do the exercise fully clothed in your imagination until your comfort level increases, focus on what part of the clothing becomes wet first. What does that feel like? Remember, this exercise is coming from your imagination. It is *yours*. Create as little or as much as you feel you can. If you feel you could not be as truthful in the exercise as you would have liked to be, remember that the next time you attempt it, it will be fuller.

8. When you have investigated as much or as little as is comfortable, turn the shower off. Do you feel yourself dripping wet? Where? Where do you still experience "cold" or "warm" on your body?

9. Physically get out of the shower. Towel yourself off using an imaginary towel.

10. Take your pad of paper and write down only the feelings you got from doing this exercise, or speak them into a tape recorder. Just describe the current feelings such as: "My arm feels cold," "My head hurts . . . it is sore just above the eyes," or "The middle of my back feels wet, but I can't feel the water on my shoulders."

Concentrate on hot and cold, wet or dry in order to actually feel and not intellectualize what you think you should feel. The experiences that come up in these exercises will begin to help you connect mind and body. For instance, a particular sensation on a part of your body might be connected to other memories surrounding that area.

The Shower Exercise is often the first time survivors allow themselves to feel the sensations in their bodies.

Karry's Story

Karry was a thirty-six-year-old African-American woman who had been married three times. Her five children had come from those three husbands, and her eldest son had been "an accident" from her husband raping her one night. He had also given her herpes as well as another curable but unsightly sexually transmitted disease, all of which kept her chaste for a year and four months. Her husband had then used her celibacy as a reason to beat her on a regular basis.

When Karry was sixteen, her mother married a man many years her senior who began to fondle the teen when the mother was away. Upon learning of her husband's "infidelity" with her daughter, the mother flew into a rage at Karry, kicked her out of the house, and refused to ever see her again. Karry became a street person, living in a pack with other street kids. At first, she found it "fun," but then soon found herself isolated and in danger.

She finally found herself retreating to a shelter for wayward teens. There for the first time, she began to experience love from people who wanted to help her.

Karry had spent most of her adult life in therapy, and by the time she came to me, her faith in it was low. But she was willing to keep trying until something worked. She was sure that doing exercises was silly and would make her laugh. At least in this therapy she planned on "having a good time." As she experimented with relaxation and the coffee cup, she found that she was fascinated by the feelings that emerged, but nothing really touched her. In fact, touch was what Karry hated most. She didn't like anyone to touch her for any reason, and she was "revolted" by the idea of feeling herself. Even boyfriends were discouraged from putting their hands on her. Sex was a separate act, one which she didn't really consider "touching."

Karry's only experience with sex had been violent. If she didn't submit to her stepfather's demands, he beat her. She grew up believing that if you don't give in to men, they will punish you. However, she found that if she complied with their wishes, she was given good things, like money, shelter, clothing, and gifts.

Karry began the Shower Exercise believing that nothing would help her feel. In her first attempt at it, she remembered a seemingly disconnected experience during the "pounding of the water" on the top of her head. It reminded her of sleeping in the street when it was raining and finding a man, a stranger, who allowed her to share shelter with him if she allowed him to touch her. She also discovered that being touched meant a certain amount of intimacy, which she had learned at an early age would inevitable turn to violence. Many times she had fought for food, clothing, and other necessities with other street children.

Because of her experiences on the street, Karry grew up with a feeling of humiliation surrounding her body.

So the Shower Exercise was a big step in her ability to accept and appreciate her physical self. During the exercise, as she allowed the water to fall where she wanted it to on her body, she was finally able to describe her physical reactions to being naked in a shower. By being able to trust the audience, me, she was also helped to begin feeling like a responsible, in-control adult person who could take care of herself.

Karry began using "the Shower Exercise" to investigate her sexuality sensorially. She found touching to be a transitional way to learn what she needed sexually. The exercise proved to be an important first step, another layer lifted in her discovery of the memories and feelings hidden in and about her body.

Chapter 6

The Fourth Wall Exercise

Overcoming Guilt

Maria looked worn out, tired, and much older than her forty years. She described herself as the "no" girl. All she heard as she grew up was "no" from her parents. She received so many negative messages from them that she became completely insecure and unsure of herself. What worried her most was not that she began to believe all these negative messages, but that she found she could not make any choices without consulting her parents first. It wasn't that she could make only bad choices—she couldn't make *any* choices. She was completely dependent on what they thought and felt.

As a child, if you were allowed freedom and opportunity to initiate playing, you probably have a strong sense of people. In sexual and other relationships, you have a sense of playfulness; you have the ability to have a good time.

However, many survivors I've worked with had parents who considered their child's self-initiated play to be a nuisance, which then caused the child to develop a sense of guilt over being an independent self-starter. That same parent is the one who finds fault with everything the child wants to investigate. This negativity can be debilitating and can further dampen your ability to make good choices for yourself in adulthood. A real sense of doubt and guilt can evolve that will continue throughout life until these feelings are contained and the reason for them resolved.

In the next exercise, the Fourth Wall, you will begin to initiate your sense of your own space; an area or place that belongs to you alone, and allows you to do whatever you want in it, free of criticism and the fear of rejection.

The Fourth Wall Exercise

The Fourth Wall Exercise is the first acting exercise that allows an actor to be "alone" in front of an audience. For a trauma and abuse survivor this is an important first step in overcoming shame and humiliation. It is also the first exercise that allows the survivor to begin making choices in front of others without their interference.

This exercise has many functions, but its main one is to help you create a safe reality. As you recreate objects and put them on your Fourth Wall, stop and allow yourself to feel what is happening in your body. This is a good mind/body exercise and one that will help you ultimately segue into the inner acting exercises. Because the Fourth Wall Exercise encompasses aspects of all the other external exercises, let's create one now.

As in this and *all* the exercises, begin with the Sunshine (Relaxation) Exercise.

1. Let your mind bring up a room, any room *except* the room or rooms where you were abused . . . at least for right now. Later, when you're used to creating places and things, you will feel more secure in creating that place, too.

2. As I will continue to suggest, always ask present-tense, action-oriented questions that will spur you on to "do" rather than simply "think." So, in your mind's eye, begin placing the furniture in the room: where do you want couches, chairs, tables, loungers, rugs, lamps, accessories, and the telephone to be in your room? If you have created a room from your past, be specific about where you want remembered objects, pictures, and sculpture to be placed: on the walls or around the room? Try to remember how they looked when you lived in this room. Or, if this is a fantasy place, think about why you are placing objects where you do.

3. You will create the fourth wall to this room last. So when you feel you have recreated the three sides to your room to the best of your memory or ability, go to the fourth wall, that space where the audience would naturally be seated. Stand there and empty your mind for a moment. Let the creativity come to you; don't try to go to it.

4. Now begin to build an imaginary wall to separate yourself from the "audience." Simply allow the wall to emerge from your unconscious mind. Let your imagination create the whole wall. Look at the wall. What kind of surface is on it: wallpaper, paint, pictures, or a window?

5. Be specific. What kinds of pictures have you placed there? How big are they? What kinds of frames do they have? How were they rendered: in oil, watercolor, or pen and ink? Are they cartoons? What do they depict? A scene in the country? A portrait?

   If your mind has brought up a child's room, the scene may depict cartoon-type characters. However, if you have created a more formal atmosphere, original oil paintings might reflect that decor.

6. If you have put a window in your wall, what kind of windowpanes does it have? Is the glass a solid pane, or has it been broken into three or four glass squares each framed by wood? Is the glass dirty or clean? Can you see clearly out of it? How big is the window? Are there curtains, drapes, blinds, shutters? Is the window open or shut?

7. What else is on your fourth wall? Can you see finger smudges or other grime? Is the paint peeling? Where? Put your hand on the wall. What do you feel? What texture? Is the texture rough or smooth? Look at the floor. How does it meet the wall? Are there baseboards? If so, what color are they?

8. What memories or thoughts come up for you as you look around the room and at the wall? Pause and ask yourself specific questions as you investigate each object. What feelings come up? Isolation, happiness, sadness, worry, insecurity? Again, the wall is *your* creation, so if you begin to become panicked or otherwise uncomfortable, end the exercise anytime you need to.

9. Go to your pad of paper or turn on your tape recorder and record all feelings and memories gleaned from this exercise.

For actors, an important aspect of creating a scene is to feel secure that their creation will not be seen by others, like an audience, until they are ready to have it seen. The Fourth Wall Exercise was devised for just that reason—the same type of separation of self and others will come to abuse survivors with this exercise.

Another useful aspect of the Fourth Wall Exercise for both abuse survivors and actors is that this exercise stimulates us to be private immediately so we can be involved with our reality and be truly aware of our needs and wants. We know others see us, watch us and are aware of us, but we need to focus on our business without being pulled out of it by the knowledge that others are out there judging us. Like actors in a role, for abuse survivors it can be quite a task to create this space. The Fourth Wall Exercise allows actors and survivors alike to concentrate on their own, personal reality alone or in public.

Once the wall is up, the audience is replaced by that imaginary wall with the objects you need to work with.

Before we go forward with more emotionally laden exercises, it might be advantageous for you, too, to create a safety zone with this useful exercise.

Petra's Story

My client, Petra, had been emotionally and sexually abused by her mother. So as an adult she tried to avoid anyone who approached her. As she reported in therapy, as a roundabout way of fending off attackers, she allowed herself to become seriously overweight. But then, ashamed of the weight, she used surgical means to have it removed. Once the weight was under control, she soon found other destructive means for expressing her fear, self-consciousness, and shame:

She became a sex addict. She sought men out for "quickies" during the afternoon. On one occasion, while on a lunch date with a girlfriend, she found herself flirting with two men, strangers, sitting at the bar. Before the meal was over, Petra had agreed to drive off with both of them, leaving her bewildered friend behind. The friend, concerned for Petra's safety, had wisely taken down the license plate numbers of the car in case Petra turned up missing.

Later that day, the friend called Petra at home only to find her drunk and crying. Apparently, the men had taken her to a motel, both had sexual relations with her, then left her at the motel to pay the bill. Petra had to call a cab to take her home. Shamed and angry, she refused to come out of her house for a week after the episode. Petra reported feeling dissociated, as if she were "out of my body"; she felt as if the person who did those sexual things was not she, but someone else.

In therapy, Petra reported that her body felt as if it belonged to everyone *but* her. Our sessions seemed to proceed very slowly at first. We spent many months talking about her experiences. The Fourth Wall Exercise was useful to her for finding her boundaries.

The Fourth Wall Exercise became her favorite because she said that until she practiced with that exercise, she had never been able to create personal and private boundaries; there always seemed to be a blur between her and other people. Petra credited her ability to create the fourth wall with helping her outline some limits between herself and others. A bonus from doing the exercise was that, as she repeated it over and over again, new objects occurred to her to put on the wall. These objects, she felt, truly defined her. The exercise seemed to work wonders for her, helping her to re-own who she was and take possession of herself and her things. She found she could set limits and say "no" to the inappropriate demands of others.

Sound complicated? It really isn't. As a survivor, your truth and reality will become stronger in the same way actors believe in their character's environment. Sexual-abuse survivors have described that when they build their fourth wall, feelings and memories of past environments have crept into their creations, which have made them feel unsafe. However, when they put windows in or hang specific pictures on their wall and take over responsibility for building it the way they wish, they feel less threatened and more in control of their environment. This control helps them feel less panicked about the memories they will allow into this space.

Chapter 7

The Atmosphere Exercise

The Time and Place: Sights and Sounds

Atmospheres, or in other words, your environment, such as your home or apartment, are places that can turn out to be dwellings where significant events occurred in your life.

By creating atmospheres, you are also creating mood. These moods may trigger emotions and memories from the past—including memories of abuse. However, the exercise allows you to have control over how much or how little of your past life you create.

The Atmosphere Exercise

1. Do the Sunshine Exercise.
2. Sit in a comfortable chair, close your eyes, and visualize a special time in your life (at least ten years ago), like a particular birthday.
3. Remember, the event must be at least seven years old so that you have the opportunity to look back on it with the memories you have about it now.
4. Begin to ask yourself: Where am I exactly? In my home with my parents? In a place I occupied alone, like a rooming house, or friend's place. Which room am I in? In the living room, dining room, or bedroom?
5. Ask yourself: What kind of air is in this place? Musty, smelly, fresh, fragrant?

6. What do I see? Ornamentation such as symbols hanging from lamps, or presents sitting on the floor or table?

7. How old am I in this place? Look at your hand and feet in this place and atmosphere—are they small? Are you a child?

8. What time comes to mind? What are you wearing? Are you in your pajamas or robe? That would tell you what time it is: morning or evening.

9. What's on your feet? Are you barefoot or are you wearing slippers? What do they look like?

10. Is this the night before a holiday or the day itself? Would there be a difference?

11. Are members of your family there—brothers, sisters, mom, dad, extended family members? What do they look like? Whose voice do you hear? From which direction is the voice or voices coming from? Or are you alone right now?

12. Look around the room in your mind's eye. Look at every part of the room or space that you can. What can you clearly see there? Get in closer and take a good look. Describe sensorially each object that is there.

13. Now take a deep breath. What do you smell? A candle burning, the musty smell of old furniture, soot, dust, or cooking? What kind of air might be on your skin?

14. How does this day make you feel inside?

15. Take out your pad or turn on your tape recorder and write down or speak out the specific memories your recall. As you speak about the day, you will be able to bring yourself back to that time so that even more memories will surface.

Atmospheres create more memories of the past than any other exercise except the Affective Memory Exercise to be described later. Like music or fragrance, an atmosphere can transform a current place into a long ago, lost time that was never dealt with sufficiently. You can connect those memories to current, similar feelings or situations.

We're all familiar with the way certain feelings from long ago can revisit you in particular situations. Well, atmospheres help you remember where you learned to act or react under particular conditions. Once you recognize your process, you can change it, alter parts of it, or keep it. But when you do, it becomes your choice and not an unconscious, knee-jerk reaction.

Like the Animal Exercise to come later, or the Shower Exercise, the Atmosphere Exercise bridges external and internal memory states together so that feelings can find a safe haven in the body and find a place to be expressed through the voice.

Chapter 8

The Building a Room Exercise

Symbolically Remodeling Your Life

Now that you can create an atmosphere, you can create a real place like a particular room. Have you ever gone back to the place where your abuse occurred? Most people dread the thought of ever attempting to do that, and it might not be such a good idea for many. Others find that their longings are to return, to make it right, to confront, to find a way that will allow them vindication, even though they are not sure how that will work.

The Building a Room Exercise will allow you freedom to express symbolically the sexual, physical, or emotional abuse you experienced as a child. Now you can overcome any warnings you received to keep quiet about it and deny it. You may have been told not to *talk*, but now you are acting, and that will give you permission to describe and remember whatever you need to at this time, in this room.

The Building a Room Exercise

It's time to get all your power back. Trauma survivors usually feel most helpless and powerless in the place where they were abused. One way of gaining control over the feelings related to that space is to recreate it, walk around in it, discover what happened there and begin to contain the feelings that arise.

Actors use the Building a Room Exercise to help them believe in the reality of a place even though they are only on a set on a sound stage. The idea is that if an actor can create from imagination and feel "real" in a room he or she has created in acting class, he or she will have no trouble believing in the truth of a room on a sound stage. Actors need to be able to put the personal objects of the character, such as clocks, pictures, furniture and familiar objects, into this space. For abuse survivors, using personal objects, which have meaning to them, help make this pretend room into something real.

1. Allow your imagination to tell you what room you are going to create. Close your eyes and say, "I need to see a room." Allow whatever room comes to mind to emerge and be created. For whatever reason, that must be the room your unconscious wishes to explore at that moment. In other words, you can't go to the room, the room comes to you. And bravo to you for believing in it and creating it for yourself.

2. Step back and, like magic, allow three walls of the room to appear in your mind's eye. The fourth wall is a space where the audience is, and you will make special pains to create objects on that wall later.

3. Stand outside the three walls you have just created and ask yourself: What room have I built? One from my home as a child? A current space? What kind of a room is it? A bedroom, playroom, bathroom, den? How large or small is it? Is it filled with things or rather empty? What color are the walls? What furniture does it contain?

4. Now physically enter the room. That's right, just take a "step" in it. Begin to walk around the space you've created as your room. Using your imagination and focus, ask yourself out loud what you have put in this room. Stop by a piece of furniture and ask yourself what it looks like. Is it an heirloom? Why is it so personal to you? Whom did it belong to before you? When did they get it? What was the occasion? A birthday, the death of a loved one?

5. Now look at the fourth wall. What have you put on it or against it? Is there a window in this room? Where is it? Go over to it. Look out of it. What does it look out on? A garden? A garage?

6. What else is in your room? Go to each object and take a good look at it. Pick it up. Create it as fully as you can, recognizing that this is only a part of your imagination, but the part that can help you remember and contain fear. And, as always, never forget the "third eye"—that part of you that always knows exactly where you really are and what you are really doing. The third eye will continue to keep you safe.

   Be aware that all previous exercises described to this point are encompassed in this exercise. The tastes, smells, sights, and sounds of your room will bring back many memories, times in your life that were significant, and remembrances of important people.

7. As in previous exercises, when you have gained as much as you can out of this exercise, go to your pad of paper, turn to a new page and write down any and all feelings you have about your room. If you're using a tape recorder, go ahead and record your feelings.

In the next chapter, we will put these exercises together for you to enter a room for a reason, and exit when your objective has been completed—or when you can do no more to resolve why you came into this place.

Chapter 9

The Entrance and Exit Exercise

Your Right to Come In

A good example of how this exercise is used in acting was a scene acted in class where an actor playing a very lonely character has taken refuge in a mountain retreat. Another actor playing good friend of his has decided to rescue the poor man by taking a trip to the cabin to talk his friend into coming back to society.

The second actor's entrance begins with his entering the cabin to help his friend out of his depression. As the actor enters, he looks around, sees where his friend is situated, and takes his cue from that as to how to proceed with his goal of helping his friend. If his friend is lying on the bed, for instance, the actor might go over to the bed to see if the fellow is asleep. He then has another hurdle. Does he wake his depressed friend or wait patiently until the man stirs? The next phase of the scene may be deep conversation as to why the fellow should come back to society in the first place. Either the friend agrees to come with the actor or doesn't. That decision will dictate how the helpful friend character exits the cabin: either with his friend, with a promise from his friend that he will come later, or with his friend refusing to ever leave.

For abuse survivors, the Entrance and Exit Exercise is a good tool to help you determine how you might contact, connect with, or confront your abuser. The entrance will depend on how fearful, guilty, angry, or dependent you feel about that person. Your exit will depend on how successful you feel your confrontation with the abuser has been. This exercise will help you begin to rehearse a confrontation with the perpetrator of your abuse.

Before you begin this exercise, consider a few questions that may help catapult you into the spirit of the exercise: Do you feel it is necessary at some time to eventually speak to, connect with, or confront your abuser? Has anything happened to you as an adult, recently or in the past, that makes you want to make contact? Will such a contact represent closure for you? Retribution? What are you expecting to get out of the confrontation, and will you be okay if you don't necessarily get that? How do you think that person will take your reentry into his or her life, probably after many years of no connection?

The Entrance and Exit Exercise

1. Think of a room, a park, a beach, a mountain trail, or any other definite place that immediately comes to mind.
2. Begin to create that place by positioning existing furniture in your environment in order to make it real for you.
3. Give yourself a reason for your presence in this place at this time. Put yourself as fully in that place as you can.
4. Begin to speak out loud. You might first ask yourself: What am I doing here? Whom am I waiting for? What do I plan to say to that person? What do I hope to accomplish before I leave this place?
5. Now put someone or something there; give yourself a reason to connect with this person right now. You might ask him or her out loud, "Why do you think I am here?" Listen to what they say and begin to do whatever you need to do to accomplish your objective, perhaps getting them to admit what they did!
6. Remember, you must succeed or fail at your chosen objective before you can leave this space.

Kathy's Story

Kathy, forty-five years old, was abandoned by her father when he abandoned her mother. He was a very flamboyant movie producer, and he had many girlfriends and many interesting people around him, so when he abandoned the family, Kathy felt completely alone, and she felt he had abandoned her. She felt she never could find the "key" to her father that she needed in order to connect with him. She didn't know how to reach him emotionally, get him to notice her, or make herself as important to him as his girlfriends had been.

She finally found the way to bond with her father when she became a teenager and began having her own boyfriends. She and her father began to create a kind of conspiracy together where she could use his expertise, learned in his own relationships, to help Kathy manipulate each of her new boyfriends into being in a relationship with her; being involved in her life due to some machination she used, thanks to her father, to entice the boy.

As an adult, she continued the dynamic of playing at "getting the guy" and really not wanting a relationship as much as she wanted to "win" him, usually away from some other woman. She wanted to win back her father from all those women who had taken him away from her. During one particularly unfortunate relationship, Kathy met a man, an aspiring producer, who she felt she could buy through all her connections in show business.

But what happened was that because she was "buying" her new lover, she realized the love she thought she was getting from him wasn't real; it wasn't truthful, and so she began to become more jealous, more possessive of him and his time, more unsure of herself. At one point she became so suspicious of him that she went down to his beach house on a day she suspected he would be entertaining an old girlfriend, sat hidden in her car outside the building, and waited until she could see them leave. She then let herself into his house with the key she had forced him to give her, went upstairs to the bedroom, and hid in the closet. Kathy wasn't sure what she was going to do, but she sat on the floor of that dark closet and waited. When she heard her boyfriend and the woman come back into the house, she noticed that she started to get very excited rather than angry. She sat almost frozen in the closet as she listened to them climb the stairs, enter the bedroom, undress, and begin to make love.

Finally, when she could stand it no more, she threw open the closet door, yelling his name. Both her boyfriend and his ex-girlfriend jumped out of the bed, shocked and stunned. But Kathy noticed she felt vindicated, that she felt powerful again. She felt that she had shown her boyfriend up for what he really was.

During the Entrance and Exit Exercise, Kathy noticed the entrance she needed to make was to confront her father about his infidelities and departure from the family, not as boldly and dramatically as she had confronted her boyfriend, but to face her father honestly and talk to him about how she felt. Even though she found she was fearful of a real confrontation with her father—she was afraid she would not be able to stand up to his furious temper and the anger she felt would come out of him as he denied his participation in leaving the family—she still wanted to let him know how hurt she felt when he left her. Her exit was her own realization that her father could either understand her position, or she would leave realizing he could never understand it. The important part of the exercise was that *she* finally accepted and understood what she needed to say directly to him, and in that way she finally came to terms with the relationship she had with her father as a child, vindicating herself. Later she was able to confront her father, and based on what she discovered about her needs in the Entrance and Exit Exercise, she found that when she left he was sorry about what had happened, which made the two of them even closer.

The Entrance and Exit Exercise helped Kathy learn to curb the feelings of being overwhelmed by her childhood. Normal psychological reactions to trauma may become exaggerated and extreme in a child's mind (as well as during adulthood). This childhood trauma can lead to adulthood panic, emotional and physical exhaustion, and even extreme avoidance of anything real. Memories may be dissociated from consciousness as you, the survivor, set up reconstructions to try desperately to remember what you believed happened to you. These recreations often come in the guise of fantasy, daydreaming, or other escapes from life. In fact, you might feel psychic numbing from real life.

For Kathy, rather than constant upheaval in her life, she began to understand that healing was stirring up old feelings of terror and powerlessness as well as anger and sadness at the loss of her father to another woman. She began to use the Entrance and Exit Exercise to work out coping strategies for times of jealousy and lack of self-respect so that she could talk out rather than act out those periods of crisis.

Chapter 10

The Mountain Exercise

Now that your imagination is used to soaring the heights, let's make up a place where you can go to find your unconscious mind. That's right, to wander (at least in your mind's eye) into the deepest, darkest part of your mind. That place where you can't really go by just wishing it. That place that holds all your emotional and "feeling" secrets: times you had that were wonderful, but forgotten; and times you had that were terrible and frightening and left you with scars that prevent you from living your life fully and with the most success you can have.

The Mountain Exercise is a visualization exercise akin to hypnosis. In fact, I use this exercise regularly when I put clients through a hypnosis experience.

Remember that you are using this exercise to allow your unconscious mind to come forward, to take you where it needs to go right now. So try not to control what happens when you travel in your mind down the dirt path, up the mountain, and into the cave at the top of the mountain.

The Mountain Exercise

1. Do the Sunshine Exercise, concentrating on all your muscle groups. Make sure you feel completely relaxed, and "empty" your mind of current, extraneous thoughts.
2. Lie down on the floor, a really comfortable couch, or a reclining chair. Take off your shoes if you wish, and make sure your clothing is loose fitting and unencumbered.
3. Close your eyes. Picture in front of you a long dirt or sand pathway. On either side of the pathway are flowers or stones.

4. Picture yourself walking down this pathway. Notice the foliage or the objects on either side.

5. Notice if you wish that the air is balmy and there is a soft wind. You can feel it on your cheeks and blowing through your hair. You have now put yourself into an altered state of being. You are still you, in the present of wherever you are doing this exercise, but your mind, your memories, and even your body are in this new state because you're focused on these images.

6. Say to yourself, "I am giving myself permission to take this journey, but if I don't like where I'm going, I will stop, open my eyes, and be in my room again."

7. Continue to walk down the pathway and notice that it is beginning to slope upward, as if up a steep hill or a mountain. In fact, it is becoming a mountain road. Keep your eyes closed.

8. Notice how you are breathing as you walk up the roadway. You can speak out loud, if you wish, and simply and softly say, "I feel the difference in my breathing from when I was walking on flat ground and my walking up a hill now."

   Notice that as you speak to yourself in the privacy of your room that the more you define where you are and what you're doing, the more you will believe in the images and the deeper you will get into your imaginary creation.

9. As you continue to climb up the mountain, the foliage is beginning to change. What were flowers on both sides of you might now be dried out grass or other flora and fauna. Just acknowledge that it is different if it is.

10. Now, in your mind's eye, look upward at the mountain. See how far you need to travel to reach the top of it. Also notice that at the top of the mountain there is a flattened terrain where there appears to be the entrance to a large cave. Look and see the mouth of that cave. Remember to ask yourself the usual questions: Is the mouth of the cave large or small? Does it appear dark inside? Can I even see that far yet. Can I see rock formations inside the cave?

11. Now, as you reach the top of the mountain, stop for a moment at the entry to the cave. Turn and look around. Can you see the valley below? What does it look like? Are there people down there? What are they doing? What is the air like up here on the mountain? Does it feel thin and hard to breathe, or are you surprised at how easy it is to breathe?

12. Focus on the entrance. Notice that directly in front of the entrance to the cave, a large monster stops you. You can do one of three things: you can

kill the monster, you can join with the monster—put him on *your* side, or you can reduce the monster to a tiny beast.

13. Now begin to walk into it. Notice how dark it is inside, but notice too how many lighted torches there are inside. You might visualize these torches as long rods on top of which a huge flame of fire emerges, illuminating the cave.

14. As you notice each part of the interior, pick up a torch and hold it in front of you. Begin to search the cave. What do you see? Are there walls of stone inside? Put the torch closer to the walls. What are they made of? Can you smell anything in here? Put your free hand out in your mind's eye and "touch" something you see inside the cave. What is it? Is it familiar? Is it something you owned now or long ago?

15. Now notice that there is an unlit part of the cave; a place where no light exists at all. In your mind's eye, take yourself to that spot and light it with the torch you are carrying. Ask yourself, "What is here? What do I see?" Whatever comes to mind is that part of your unconscious that may have been hidden, partially hidden, or even feared until now.

16. Is there a shelf, an object, a memory in this darkest of corners? If it is tangible, pick it up. Feel it, speak out loud, and describe the object and what it means to you. Now carefully put it back. Or perhaps you wish to take the object back with you to the present.

17. Look around the cave one more time, go to the place where you first picked up the torch, return the torch and move toward the exit of the cave. Perhaps you turn one more time to look at the interior, but you know you can return whenever you want.

18. Begin to walk down the path, noticing again that this is a downward slope. How does that feel? Find yourself on the flat path again, notice the flowers or stones, the sand, dirt, or trees.

19. Now say, "I am returning to the present." Open your eyes.

20. Write in your notebook or pick up your tape recorder and just describe the feelings you have right now, including any memories from the past or anything that occurs to you now.

This trip into your unconscious mind comes from allowing yourself to look at the deepest, darkest corner of the mountain cave. You may discover now that other memories connected to whatever you found in the mountain may come forward or that the next time you do the exercise other thoughts, wishes, or memories will emerge. In any case, you have just allowed yourself to open up to whatever is really on your mind.

Part Three

The Internal Exercises and How They Work

Chapter 11

The Internal Acting Exercises and How They Work

When we began the external acting exercises, I explained how, by creating your external environment and putting objects into it, you would begin to feel long repressed feelings. Remember that the external acting exercises have to do with creating an atmosphere where you can begin to remember what happened to you, the circumstances surrounding your abuse, and any other information that will help you recover from your trauma. The external acting exercises use time and place very much in the way directors of old-time movies filled the screen with images of pages falling fast from a calendar or clouds hurrying by in the sky as indications that time is passing by quickly.

Externally creating a space can bring back memories of music, sounds, voices, scents, and other long-repressed unconscious material that is important to integrate the feelings surrounding abuse. Remember, as unconscious feelings come into consciousness, they are felt, identified, and then they automatically change.

The internal exercises act exactly the opposite from the external ones. Now, instead of creating an environment to elicit feelings, you will create the feelings first, then be reminded of the environment that went along with those feelings. At the same time you will also trigger memories of the people and objects that were important to you in your childhood. So remember, this journey of healing began first with your creating environments to dig up feelings, and now you will create feeling states to remember people and places. You will begin to help yourself solder together any fragmentation of your body and mind.

You might notice first how objects always seem to be in the middle of this paradigm. This is not an arbitrary happening. Objects are the most important tool we have to bring our unconscious minds into consciousness. They allow us to really remember smells, tastes, sights, thoughts, and sounds—only now as adults, not children. Objects act as conduits to eliciting inner feelings, naming them, and then losing fear of these feelings by experiencing them as mature adults.

You, as an adult, then have the opportunity to explore what you want to do with all that anger, shame, and need for confrontation and revenge. Perhaps you can transform those feelings into productive ways of expression that may include confronting your abuser or exposing other abusers. In any case, once the senses become awakened with the internal acting exercises, you may discover that in your life right now hidden abuse fantasies still crop up when you masturbate or have sex. They may disgust you, but you might worry that these fantasies are the only way you will ever be able to experience sex. We are going to use the internal exercises to dispel that fear.

As you begin to create feeling states, keep in mind that you are in control of how far you want to go. Many memories of where you first encountered these feelings will give you a new ability to connect these emotions to your body. You will be able to discuss your feelings rather than hide them, and you will find that these exercises help you develop a comfort level where you can remember feelings without experiencing panic.

Recovering Forgotten Memories Safely

The much-disputed concept of whether or not we harbor repressed memory has already been partially resolved by abuse survivors who report that their bodies respond in different ways from their minds. The body does remember what happened to it. And, at this point, the feelings that have come up by using the external exercises have probably helped you bring up lots of memories and thoughts about your past abuse. You probably have written down many of those feelings by now, and memories will continue to surface. If you have no idea where all this emotion is coming from, you are at least aware that *you* are creating situations that are awakening memories. This ability to recreate memories and bring up feelings is a very important tool that will allow you to identify emotions that come up due to the abuse instead of having those feelings confuse and control you.

When Freud described recreating familiar childhood patterns in adulthood, he called his discovery "repetition compulsion." He wrote that we unconsciously recreate the same patterns, even abusive ones, in our current functioning in order to try to resolve them. Perhaps we feel that by doing the same thing over and over again, the pattern will become so boring it will finally magically stop. But it simply doesn't work that way. Unfortunately, too often we do not even recognize these old patterns in current situations as being the same type of abuse that occurred in the past.

For instance, during sexual encounters in the present, some abusive repetitions may occur that we experienced in the past. However, we might feel that these are out of our control and wonder where they ever came from. We don't recognize the abuse as the same relationship we had with mother, father, or even an old boyfriend.

A client of mine came back to therapy after each new relationship went sour. She couldn't recognize that she hooked up with the same type of man time after time: an asexual, control freak. She wanted to blame her partners each time she broke up with one of them, but somewhere inside she knew her attracting this type of person was out of her control. She needed to find out where the desire to be with this type of man came from. She finally did bring up a past incident that seemed to be the beginning of cruel relationships when she discovered that her father had always told her no man would ever be as good to her as he was. She deliberately found men who would confirm that prediction. What a relief when she created a time in her childhood when daddy put her to bed, read her a story, and promised her he would provide for her forever. Now, in her adulthood, she was determined to find an equal partner and fulfill her need to be part of a team, not someone who was only capable of depending on a man.

Abuse Patterns During Sex

Abuse patterns often come out during adult sexual encounters. We allow others to be inappropriate either physically or verbally during or after sex. Or perhaps sex itself appears dirty or abusive, and we can't enjoy ourselves without recreating some kind of pain. Then, to our horror, the same emotions may come up during an adult sex act that were experienced during the abuse in childhood.

Another client of mine cried that every boyfriend eventually became just like her father. Survivors initially feel powerless over these confused sexual feelings and, in order not to feel the same sensations they experienced when they were molested in childhood, they withhold any feelings from their partner in adulthood; they mute their feelings so as not to be disgusted all over again. These are some of the feelings we want to gain control over.

Abuse Patterns in Life

I remember once calling a plumber to come up to fix a faucet. He gave me a date—and didn't show up. We made another appointment, and the same thing happened. Then, when I called to see why he hadn't showed, he told me that when I had more extensive problems to give him a call. That kind of behavior is abusive. Often we don't label it as such, but abuse it is, and the minute you feel that you're being treated abusively it is up to you to confront this treatment. The internal acting exercises will help you recognize when you are being used, abused, and manipulated.

In the above case, I called the man back and told him his behavior was abusive, and that I wouldn't be using him ever. That felt good—not so much in telling him off, but rather for having the ability, finally, to recognize abuse, nip it in the bud, and confront an abusive person.

Emotional Release Work Through Acting

As I stated above, our bodies contain the emotional memories from specific abuses. These emotions come out at the most unexpected times and appear not to be related to what is happening right now. By confronting these emotions, we gain confidence and self-assurance. We can no longer feel ruled by them.

As you begin now to look inward, you will need to trust yourself that you can risk feeling the old abuse, but will not be reabused. This time you will understand and control what happened, how it happened, and how it has left you feeling today. Although, as we have said, trust is something abuse survivors have in small amounts, you may find to your delight that you can trust yourself, because as each exercise helps you unfold a deeper feeling, you will experience that feeling in this moment as an adult. You will find yourself trusting your instincts. You will no longer be acting, thinking, or emotionally responding the way you know the abuser wanted you to. You will be developing your own sense of being in the world.

Remembering the Abuse and Expressing Yourself

We are going to use the internal exercises to help you tease apart the old feelings of anger and disgust from new, hopeful anticipation. These old feelings may have become compounded by years of anger and frustration that are all coming back in everything you do. As you strengthen your ability to connect your mind to your body without feelings of despair, disgust, or fear, you may be surprised at how fast your anger dissipates. As you help old memories to come forth through these inner exercises where taste, touch, sound, smell, and sight are used to remember, you will also have a concurrent sensation in your body. Be aware of that bodily reaction. Then your mind and your body will begin connecting your memories into a cohesive whole so that you can safely reexperience the fear you felt as a child and let it go. Involve yourself with these connections and allow them to take hold to whatever degree you are able at the moment. You will be surprised at how easily your feelings will come to you.

What Is the Internal Experience Like?

With the internal exercises, you are now going to use what we call sensory objects to really experience your inner emotional life. The emotions that emerge can be very spiritual experiences and ones that allow you to finally feel that you own your own body.

Have you ever watched a movie where someone has died and his or her lover comes into the bedroom, looks at the dead character, and then picks up a special thing or object that was part of the deceased person's life? Perhaps a perfume bottle with the scent the late person wore or an article of their clothing is taken. Each object should be important to the lover, because that thing will connect the lover to the dead character. In acting, actors must use props scattered about the room placed there by the set decorator. The actor handling them must imbue them with personal meaning in order to get the emotions necessary for the scene to play well.

A story that was a favorite in my acting class (I don't know how true it is) was of a great actor who played Hamlet. During the scene where he says, "Alas, poor Yorick! I knew him, Horatio," this actor actually used the real skull of his dead son!

For my money, that's a bit much. But actors can uncover their true emotions through objects—some real, some imaginary. So, as you can see, it is very important for actors to have a number of personal objects on hand that have particular meaning, and that will allow them a rich variety of feelings from which to choose. Real emotions emanating from objects add depth and truthfulness to performances.

As I said, in order to achieve the emotional highs and lows needed for a scene an actor needs to imbue these commodities with his or her own meaning so that an audience will be moved by the actor and believe he or she has real feelings for the object he or she is holding. So, in the hands of an accomplished performer a ten-cent comb from the set designer becomes a diamond tiara; the actor's hairbrush becomes a magic wand.

For abuse survivors, creating objects out of imagination or using real objects from the past helps mediate similar experiences today. Instead of the fear you once felt, you might now be furiously angry or sad. By conjuring up real feelings, you will lose your fear of them—you will be facing them head on. Inner emotional work has been described by many authors today as finding the inner child or discovering the "spiritual you." Survivors can accomplish the same tasks through action, and action consists of using real, tangible things to discover real emotions.

Let's look at some internal exercises that will help you discover your "feeling" life.

Chapter 12

The Sense-Memory Exercise

The Secret Is in My Senses

Earlier exercises built on your sense memories of time, place, space, and atmosphere. Using your five senses, you slowly yet surely recreated the past and began to reexperience the circumstances surrounding your abuse. Specific places and objects helped you gain access to deeper memories. Now you are ready to connect these memories with body sensations that you have been experiencing throughout the years; sensations for which you didn't know the source.

One of the more frightening and discomfiting aftereffects of any kind of child abuse is dissociative disorder. Dissociation is described as a change in your consciousness, memory, identity, or perception. It can feel as if you are "absent" or in a dream, ready to wake up but unable to. It's like being "out of" your body and not really able to feel whole. It can have very scary effects, because most people who experience dissociation are puzzled by how quickly and automatically the aftereffect can hit them.

My client Lily was terrified one evening when she came out of the movies with two good friends soon after her father had passed away. When the movie ended and the three left the theater, Lily suddenly felt as if she were "totally out of my body . . . like I was absent . . . in a dream." She reported feeling "surreal" and that she had lost all control, she thought, over her body. She described it like "trying to wake up from a nightmare and being unable to."

The Sense-Memory Exercise helped Lily use her environment to control her inner terror. This exercise is a direct way to begin your internal odyssey into exploring how dissociation and derealization (the feeling that you are not you) can come about and how you can gain control over them. The exercise is also a good tool to help you discover where in your body repressed memories are contained. You will learn how fantasy contributes to feelings of derealization and dissociation, and how masturbation can bring up the abuse while disguising it as sex. You will also begin to understand where you feel sick in your body and how you use your body to protect yourself from unwanted memories.

You will use personal objects that have "history" for you, such as a particular ring, bracelet, piece of clothing, or picture that stirs your emotions and gets your imagination flowing. You have already done some of this work in other exercises such as the Build a Room and Portrait exercises. Now you will be teasing apart the nuances of feeling that come up for you.

An Example of Using a Sense-Memory Exercise

When I first began exploring with the Sense-Memory Exercise, I used the memory and recreation of my father's favorite object, which was his own father's watch. It looked like the kind Theodore Roosevelt used to wear: a large, round, vest watch with prominent numbers and an old-fashioned second hand. There was an inscription on the smooth silver back of the watch that had all but worn off, so only the year "1921" could be seen. This became my father's timepiece; he was never without it. When my father died, my brother inherited the watch (I wouldn't have known what to do with a man's chain-hanging timepiece), and I never saw it again.

But the memory of the watch was embedded in my mind and the symbolism and reminders of my father with it. And, because of my close relationship with my father, the watch still had special memories for me. Whenever I acted and played a role where I needed to find wistful, sad, or contemplative feelings, I made the watch my imaginary object.

I always experienced the true emotions I felt for my father whenever I tried to remember the smell, feel, and look of the watch. This imaginary recreation of something that belonged to my deceased father always brought me warm feelings laced with nostalgia of many wonderful times being with him and playing with him: going to Blum's candies or watching the prize fights from Madison Square Garden at the Telenews Theater in San Francisco.

However, for adult survivors of abuse emotions are stunted at the age when the abuse first took place. A sensory object will not contain warm, fuzzy memories. That is why the buildup to using these objects has been so important. Survivors may complain that they have no adult identity, that they are frozen in childish fantasies, or hiding in escape behaviors to protect themselves. But for abuse survivors, these sense memories will trigger inward emotions that can bring together the time, place, people, and circumstances needed to finally overcome trauma.

You can then use your long-forgotten memories as your tool to integrate past feelings with present ones. What does that mean? It means experiencing the old feelings now as an adult, which automatically allows you to take care of yourself. No longer feeling hopeless, helpless, and frightened, but with ideas and plans of how you can now protect yourself and your family from abuse. In other words, you give yourself your power back.

As you identify emotions from the past that emanate from these sensory objects, you will notice how you respond to them in the present. And since you deliberately conjured them up, you will be able to control them along with the panic that may be brought up with them.

The Sense-Memory Exercise

1. Find an object from your past. It does not have to be imaginary, although it can be. I prefer now to use real objects in my environment like a ring or an anniversary present from my husband. Just make it personal, not something generic like a coffee cup. You may have a coffee cup that has strong meaning for you, so definitely use it if that is true. However, if it does not hold special emotional content or is not from a crucial time in your life, pick something else that is.

   Perhaps your object will be a gift your parents left you such as a doll, a train, a piece of jewelry, or it may be another favorite object that holds tons of memories and feelings. Whenever I discussed any object with my acting coach, Jack Garfein, he would say, "Now tell me when you got it." That brought up a slew of memories surrounding the present and the moment I received it.

2. As you have done in the other exercises, pick up the object and look at it from all sides. Do you remember when you got it? Was it a present from someone? Whom? Under what circumstances did you get it? Who was there? Where were you when you received it?

3. Feel the object. Is it smooth, silky, soft, furry, hard, crumbly? What kind of a texture does it have?

4. Smell it. Does it have a smell? Is it a musty smell from years ago?

5. Look at it. Is it shiny? Dull? Muted? What color or colors does it contain? Is one color predominant? Does it have a face? What color are the eyes? What is the object wearing? Describe it sensorially, by texture, color, and feel.

6. Can you taste it? Is it appropriate to taste it? I once found myself licking a sweater to see how wool would feel on my tongue. I found that the taste was cotton-like. It reminded me of times I had been too shy to speak and had felt cotton-mouthed. So it turned out to be a useful investigation.

7. Do noises emanate from your object? Describe those noises. As you play with the object, can you hear anything from it at all?

8. Now just deal with the object. Identify your feelings, all of them—no matter what they are. Perhaps you don't remember everything; so what especially sticks out in your mind? Just let any and all feelings come up.
9. Now add to your feelings by describing how your body feels right now.
10. Speak your experience into your tape recorder or write down what you have discovered. Is there tightness or pain anywhere? What exactly does that feel like? Is there anything else about the object that you think might be a pertinent residual of your exercise?

Use Your Senses to Control Dissociation

The Sense-Memory Exercise is the exercise you will use to overcome dissociation if you do have episodes of splitting mind from body or feelings of derealization. In the exercise that follows, notice that you need to be concrete and specific as you begin to smell, see, hear, touch, and taste the sensory object you have chosen to recreate. A good example of how to use the Sense-Memory Exercise when you feel absent is to use a main technique actors use to help themselves overcome disabling stage fright. If frightening feelings of dissociation appear, begin to immediately concentrate on objects *directly* next to you or beneath you, such as a rug. If you decide to use a rug to help you regain control over dissociative feelings, remove your shoes and socks and allow your feet to really deal with the texture of the rug and the feeling of the carpet material on your skin.

Ask yourself your usual, specific questions such as: What type of texture do I feel? Is it nubby or smooth? Do my feet slide easily over the rug, or do I feel ridges when I glide the soles of my feet along the carpet?

Remember to always make your answers as specific and detailed as you can. In that way you will take your concentration off of your fear and dissociation and put your focus on something real in your life, which will bring you back to reality and a sense of completeness. The more involved you become in answering your questions fully, the less panic and fear you will experience. Your concentration is immediately directed to outside stimuli that take you out of anxiety and put you in the real world. Concentration is a great control tool.

Try not to demand too much of yourself. Psychotherapy is an unfolding process and it works slowly even when questions and recollections flood your mind. However, actors and other artists regularly do these exercises, sometimes on a daily basis, to "work their emotional bodies." They don't "freak out" or have undue responses, and neither will you. If you are able to use your five senses, you will be making yourself more aware of what you are naturally doing in your life right now. So take your time in recreating your memory objects, and each memory will build on the last until you have uncovered your life experiences in a way that enables you to accept them and contain your fear of them in the present.

Each time you do this exercise, more details about your object and the circumstances surrounding it will surface, so again take your time. You will be doing this particular exercise over and over again with different objects. It will really help you deal with old memories and emotions. Some of your reactions to certain objects may surprise you—you may not have thought that you'd react that way. Allow yourself to focus on all the feeling elements.

Many abuse survivors are afraid of finding out exactly what happened and hope that "things will just work themselves out." As you probably know, that rarely happens. We need to rediscover what happened so that the secret is no longer a secret, so that you will be able to confront (or not) your abuser, and so you can form solid, loving relationships. Relinquishing your fantasy life and facing reality will help you achieve what therapy has to offer: self-actualization and a successful and happy life. The Sense-Memory Exercise is a powerful tool in aiding in your discovery of the circumstances around your abuse. These memories will fuel honesty and your ability to realize that you can have power over feelings—that you can feel, and you no longer have to hide.

Chapter 13

The Portrait Exercise

Creating a Whole, Living Person

The Portrait Exercise helps actors learn to create a whole, living person from one-dimensional material, usually a picture in a magazine or a portrait in a gallery. In this exercise, you are actually invited to use your imagination in order to decide what you think might be happening to the person in the picture, "read the mind" of the artist, and anticipate what you think might happen next to the person in the portrait after the picture is painted.

The Portrait Exercise is the best exercise I know to help survivors recognize how they wish they really could be. It also helps them pinpoint when they are anticipating fear and reacting to it before anything has even occurred. The Portrait Exercise offers the extra perk of allowing you to begin to recognize and differentiate your personality from other people's personalities, a necessary step in creating a new life. For survivors that is a definite necessity.

Because survivors were so tied to the abuser's thoughts and beliefs, they cannot extricate other people's belief system from their own. In the Portrait Exercise we begin to contrast ourselves from the person in the portrait, and in so doing, begin to differentiate ourselves from the abuser. This separation can mark the beginning of our ability to empathize with others, of seeing them as separate entities, and a lot of anxiety and anger about the way other people act toward us can be dissipated.

The Portrait Exercise allows your creativity to manifest itself to its fullest. For abuse survivors, that ability allows you to discover for yourself how you see yourself, which is your next stage of recovery.

The Portrait Exercise

1. Choose a picture, either a portrait or photo from a magazine, book, your personal collection, or by visiting a gallery or museum. If you have chosen to search through museums and galleries for your picture and have picked a well-known portrait by a master such as Degas (a favorite choice among actresses), you can go to the gallery's gift shop and purchase a postcard or print of the portrait. Then, when you get home, you can study it further, at your leisure, until you feel you have captured the picture's essence. Or, as one industrious actor friend of mine used to do, take a pencil and drawing pad with you to the museum, sit down, and sketch the painting.

2. The picture must be a portrait of a person who hopefully looks somewhat like you. And the picture should hold some meaning for you. It really doesn't matter which era or century the portrait comes from (it can be contemporary), but it should be one where you can tell what the picture is about. It must be a straightforward, recognizable portrait of someone, not a surrealistic impression.

3. Study the person in the picture. What is he or she doing? Are they standing or sitting? Are they inside a room or outside in a garden? What are they involved in doing?

4. Slowly begin to take the pose of the person in the picture. Try to position your body into the exact stance of that person. If they are holding a letter or phone, you hold a letter or phone the same way they are.

5. Freeze yourself in that position for a few seconds and become comfortable with the pose and the objects.

6. Now, *make that person become alive through your actions.* Become the person in the picture. Slowly begin to move the way you think the person in the picture might move. What do you imagine that person in the photo will do right after this pose? Go ahead and do that action and whatever movements or actions that come next.

   The idea is to take in everything you see in the drawing and consider what you imagine the person in that portrait would continue to do if he or she were alive. As you begin to break your pose, ask yourself, "What will this person do from here?"

7. Create whatever you believe the character would do now that the picture is over.

8. Go to your pad of paper or turn on your tape recorder and record any and all feelings that came up during and after this exercise.

One favorite portrait used for the Portrait Exercise in my acting class was a famous seventeenth-century work of a woman standing by an open window reading a letter. Lee Strasberg used to ask us, "What do you imagine will happen to this character when she has finished reading?" Other questions he'd ask were, "Do you think she will sit down and muse about the contents of the note?" "What do you think is *in* that letter?" "Is it happy news or sad?" "Is it a love letter? Or a telegram from the King's Court announcing the death of her lover or husband who is an officer in the army? Or a letter from a long, lost relative?" "Do you think she will burst into tears when she has finished reading it?" "Do you think she will write a reply?"

In other words, let yourself go. If you have chosen this painting, read the letter and react to whatever you have chosen it to be. If it is a letter from the character's sister, what do you imagine the sister is saying? How do you, as the character in the portrait, feel about that? That is what we are looking for—making the picture come alive by imagining the next moments after the picture was completed.

By recreating where the person in the portrait was or what they were doing just before opening the letter and reading it, you will be able to decide his or her fate after finishing it. Where do you think you, as the character in the painting, will put the letter when you are finished with it? Then what will you do? Do you, as the character, think you might go back to the same activity you were doing before you read the letter, or have the contents of the letter changed your mood so that you can't return to your prior activity? Begin to act out that action.

Actors I knew came to class prepared with elaborate costumes from a company in Hollywood that specialized in motion-picture dress design. They would duplicate the attire of the person in the portrait *exactly*. Even their makeup and personal objects were the precise look of the character in the picture—and at considerable expense to the actor. Some zealous performers not only recreated the costume, but found the props used in the picture and purchased them from a studio lot! Others made the clothes themselves to immerse themselves in the characterization of the portrait. So, this exercise can be fun as well as therapeutic.

If you have chosen a picture in which animals appear with a person, if there are other objects that cannot be duplicated effectively, or if the scene in your portrait takes place outdoors in a park or street, obviously you will have to position some chairs so that they will substitute for your "animal," "bench," or "trees."

Gloria's Story

Gloria couldn't explain why she felt so belittled, humiliated, and tortured as a child. As an adult, she felt shy, unable to speak up when she needed to, and afraid to involve herself with anyone. She lived alone, worked in a high-rise in Los Angeles, and did very little socializing. She came to therapy because she had been fired from a good job in a firm where she had worked for ten years. At fifty-two years old, she felt she was being replaced by someone younger who would command a smaller salary.

Gloria had a small savings account left by her mother, but that would not last her the rest of her life. She wasn't bad at investing, either. She was simply lonely, sad, and desperate. Anyone who even appeared slightly kind toward her was immediately put on a pedestal where Gloria looked up to them and literally used them as a role model.

In therapy she began to unravel the story of her life with acting exercises. As each external exercise reminded her more and more of her past and her childhood, she began to remember subtle swipes her family made at her self-esteem. She was told that she would never amount to anything and that she wasn't as beautiful as her mother, and she was made to feel that whatever she did not only wasn't good enough, but was actually worthless and petty.

One particularly painful memory came from the first Portrait Exercise Gloria did. She found a picture of a young woman getting dressed for a party. Gloria remembered a time she was dressing for a special occasion. Her mother had actually picked out the dress, but once Gloria put it on and was ready to go to the affair, her mother suddenly and for no apparent reason said, "You look too nice," and without warning picked up a can of spray paint she'd been using in the backyard and sprayed Gloria with it. The child was soaked with paint, too shocked to cry; in a trance-like state, she went upstairs and changed. Gloria remembered that she and her mother then went to the party without a word spoken about the incident!

When Gloria did the Portrait Exercise a second time, she used Edvard Munch's painting *The Scream*. That is the famous painting depicting a ghost-like character standing on a bridge with its mouth stretched open. Gloria took that position, opened her mouth, and froze. I watched as she created the pose, and I knew tremendous feeling was happening inside Gloria, because I could feel the hairs in the back of my neck become stiff as she worked on the exercise. Then, suddenly, she just began screaming and "running" down "the bridge" with her arms flailing. Needless to say, that "ghost" came alive for her, and all the feelings she had hidden surrounding that terrible assault were finally released so that she could feel her anger and sorrow and finally let it go.

Survivors with physical or verbal abuse histories often grow up in homes where shouting, name-calling, and rage are expressed. Communication on any calm level doesn't exist. As Gloria finished her exercise, sat on the stage, and faced me, she described the feelings that came up for her: they were of fleeing. "I suddenly remembered what my 'ghosts' were running away from. My parents locked me and my brothers in closets for hours, sometimes didn't speak to us for days, and often never expressed any feelings at all. I never knew if I was loved or hated. I still don't. And now, as an adult, I don't know whether people really like me or not. I'm always prepared for people I truly like, love even, to suddenly and for no reason at all, tell me they are leaving the country or the city and that I'll never see them again. That simply wouldn't surprise me, and I wouldn't feel bad. You see, I can't afford to."

The Portrait Exercise is very useful for survivors of child abuse because it is a tool that allows you to use your intellect to begin to *feel*. The exercise is often the first time an imaginary person is used to connect to feelings about real people from the past. As I said before, many abuse survivors use the defense of intellectualization to numb feelings. With this exercise, you can use your intellect to help you get down to your true emotions.

Even if you first create the person in the portrait intellectually, you will eventually give yourself up to the feelings that person in the portrait is evoking in you. You have created the situation, and you can react first with your head, then with your body. It is powerful, and it works!

Once you begin to combine mind and body feeling states, you will be able to differentiate how you really felt during a particular trauma as opposed to how you were told you *should* feel about it. Again, this is a way to gain back long-lost control over your emotions. As an example, consider Marta, whose father died when she was a young teen. Her mother was unable to deal with the immense pain of losing her husband, so when Marta began crying over the loss of her dad, her mother, instead of being able to be consoling, got furious with Marta. Marta was made to stop crying and be stoical the way the mother needed her to be at that time. Only after recreating a Portrait Exercise of a young woman looking over her father's coffin was Marta able to deal with the real emotions and feelings she had had over her own father's death.

Chapter 14

The History Exercise

Using Your History

It is so hard to remember most abuses, whether they are physical, sexual, emotional, or verbal. The mind uses strong coping mechanisms to deliberately spare us and keep us safe from the memories of what happened. The body remembers the way you like or don't like to be touched, kissed, or approached. It all has to do with what happened to you in childhood. Often you may find yourself reliving the trauma and then being in denial of it: intruding thoughts and numbing responses.

Escape is paramount in many of these reactions—at least you can have a good life, the life you really want, in fantasy. Because a fantasy life is so powerful and prevalent in abuse survivors' lives, this next exercise makes use of this special gift in order to aid you in overcoming dissociation, flashback episodes, or intense psychological distress over the traumatizing events in your past. And, as a bonus, the exercise helps in discovering what you unconsciously want in your life now. You will create a story around a person to uncover your true desires for yourself.

This exercise can be considered an extension of the Portrait Exercise, because now you are going to pick someone you barely know and make up a history about him or her. Actors do this exercise to enhance and enrich what their dialogue says about their characters. It is one of the most important exercises for actors since it involves understanding the life of the character: not just where they physically came from, but who they are inside, what they want, how they think, and how they live their lives on a day-to-day basis. As actors, we learn about our character through his dialogue, what he tells us about himself, and his way of being in the world.

For abuse survivors, the same holds true. By noticing your behavior—what you are doing, saying, feeling at any given time—you will better understand how you truly feel at any given time. By using your own history, it will all come together for you. First, create a stranger's history, then create your own!

The History Exercise

Test out your fantasy life. Make sure you know something about this person so that you can build on his or her true character as much as possible. I'd like you to really look at someone else: see all their characteristics so that you can distinguish what is real about the person and what is strictly a figment of your imagination.

1. Find someone in your workplace or private life right now. Perhaps you chose the guy who works steadily every day at your local café making cappuccinos. He's probably perfect!

2. Whomever you have chosen, begin to study him or her. Notice (in the case of the cappuccino maker) how he or she holds objects like the coffee, the mugs; how he or she puts the coffee in the machine and turns it on.

3. Look at what he or she is wearing under the uniform, if you can see that; otherwise, imagine what that person might be wearing. What about that person tells you that? How is he groomed? Neatly? Good haircut? Clean nails? Grooming is a good tipoff of where someone might be from or at least how they feel about themselves.

4. Now begin to make up your history about this person based on what you think you see. Begin with, "Where do I think he came from?" If he has a regional accent, you might guess the south or north or even another country.

5. Continue with, "What kind of parents do I think he has? Are they easy-going types, ridiculing, demanding? What about him (or her) tells me that?" You might notice, for instance, that the person is particularly fussy, or compulsive. Practically every grain of coffee is accounted for. Or, maybe he or she is messy. You asked for a pound of coffee to take home and they gave you a little extra.

6. Ask yourself, "Is this the type of person who has an easy time of making friends or lovers? How do I know that or suspect it?"

7. Does he or she seem shy or like they come from a lot of money or poverty? What do you suspect his or her father or mother did for a living? Why do you think that? What about the person tells you that?

8. How about education? You can probably make a pretty good guess about how much education a person has had by their grammar and way of using language. If you have the opportunity to talk further to the person, their information about current events will tip you off to how much they know.

9. Do you think this person is putting him or herself through school? Are they even interested in continuing their education, perhaps with graduate school, or do they have some other aim? In Los Angeles, lots of waiters and trainers are would-be and even working actors. Does your person look like one of these?

10. Notice the person's personality. Will they make it? Are they someone who engenders help from others? Are they likable? Are they brash and hard to be with? What tells you that?

11. Now, write down or speak into a tape recorder everything you can about what you imagine this person is really like.

The fun part of this exercise for survivors and for actors is discovering whether or not they were right. In the case of actors, because they are creating a character, they might not always be able to ask the real person if they "hit" it correctly unless they are playing a real person based on a real story. But abuse survivors can go back to the person whose "history" they are imagining and get a pretty good idea of how close—or not—they came to the truth.

So, the next time you get your cappuccino (or wherever you found your "history" subject) ask him or her about themselves. Not all the questions, just a few key ones. See if you're on the mark. You might be! But you may have it all wrong. That can be a very good thing. It will allow you to realize that you really don't know anybody until you give him or her a chance to present themselves to you.

Now, put down your own history. You can do that with a "time-line." Just draw a line across a piece of legal-sized paper. Start with the year of your birth and go up the time line chronologically all the main highlights of your life. See what you remember, what year it was, and then take a look at what you have found. Your reality will enable you to know yourself and how you became yourself better than you can ever imagine.

In a love relationship, this point is crucial. Falling in love with a real person whose personality you made up in your imagination can only cause you grief and disappointment. But abuse survivors often feel safest when they do just that. A real relationship may just feel too uncontrollable. But it's always wiser (and sexier) to discover who someone is before you put a fantasy around them.

Chapter 15

The "As If" Exercise

The Way It Could Have Been

It can be very difficult to believe that the people who were supposed to love you allowed you to be hurt as a child. It can be very difficult to talk against the people we were supposed to love, our parents and caregivers. A great deal of guilt can prevent us from dealing with how angry we are. Part of our "not remembering" is a safety valve for alleviating the guilt we sometimes feel at blaming them for what they did.

But what if you spoke out about the abuse? What would have happened to you then? What would happen to you now? The "As If" Exercise is really a problem-solving technique that allows you to investigate what you would have liked to do to stop the abuse. Now, as an adult, what would you do to protect a child, even *yourself* as a child? This exercise helps you look at how you solve current problems. In a way you have already created the As If Exercise in previous exercises.

However, using the As If Exercise by itself can be a very useful way of rehearsing how you would like to see yourself in your real world. This exercise has the added quality of allowing you to change solutions safely each time you rehearse. By working out different ways of dealing with a problem, you will eventually discover a comfortable solution to it. Actors do the As If Exercise to help them believe in their character's circumstances.

You need to be in control of that part of your life that you *can* control. The As If Exercise's effects are twofold: first, it allows you the ability to control acting-out behavior in the safety of a made-up scene; and second, it allows you to control your emerging emotions by changing circumstances as you need, in your imagination. The emotions don't control you; you control them and the situation surrounding them.

Actors use the As If Exercise for many objects and materials. For instance, acting as if the floor were made entirely of hardened straw. Try it, then stomp around in it, fall in the areas where the straw has created a hidden hole, feel how your feet would feel walking on the hardened areas of compacted straw. Some people create a snowy floor or make it a lake that has frozen over. They walk gingerly in tiny little steps so as not to slip through the ice or fall on their backsides.

The "As If" Exercise

1. First, do the Sunshine Exercise as a relaxation exercise.

2. Take any object in the room or create an imaginary object and turn that object into something completely different from what it is. A favorite metamorphosis is turning a chair into a chocolate chair. In this exercise, I like to take a chair and treat it "as if" it were made entirely of melting chocolate. First, I feel where the chair is sticky, and where the chocolate has hardened. I taste the chair. Is it milk or dark chocolate? You don't have to ever actually put your tongue on the object. Remember to always keep "touch" about a one-half inch above the surface of the object itself.

3. Remember to ask yourself the questions, "Is it melting?" "Is it becoming hard?" "Is it made out of a smelly material?"

4. Go with your imagination completely. If you have created a chair, draw your fingers about one-half inch above and across where the armrest should be, then put your fingers near your nose. Does the chair have a musty smell? Is the chair made out of some kind of food? What does that taste like? Are parts of it in the sunshine so that it spoils? Are parts of it very cold so that the food turns another color?

5. If you have created another object, perhaps one you could talk to like the face of a clock, what would it say, how would it react? Some people use a clock to create a face that is singing. Others have used all the items in their room as if they were upside down but the person is right side up. What objects are you banging into? How do you feel working with upside-down objects?

6. Use your senses of sight, sound, taste, touch, and smell to react to your object as if it were the new material.

7. Go to your pad of paper and write down any and all feelings that come up.

This exercise can really feel like an *Outer Limits* experience. The As If Exercise gives you permission to create whatever you wish and then enables you to react to it. Instead of continuing in a controlled, rigid way of thinking and feeling, this exercise allows you an opportunity to get out of the rut and allow your imagination to soar. The ability to regulate your own feelings and not be controlled by them is most powerful with this exercise.

A Russian Tragedy

The most glaring example of the power of the As If Exercise came to me when I was acting in a production of a heavy Russian play with lots of tragedy that could not be created readily or immediately from my inner feelings. If anything, so many terrible things were happening to all the characters at once that it was comical!

The story line ran something along the lines of a mother, father, and baby living in Russia who had nothing to eat one winter. The father decided to rob a bank to bring some money home. The scene opens with the father rushing on to the stage excitedly calling out to the mother, who is in the bathroom washing the baby in the bathtub.

He calls out that he has stolen the loot; he opens the bags he's brought in and begins to count money in front of the fireplace, where a raging fire has been lit. In the middle of his counting, a large wind comes up and blows the money into the fireplace. The father screams and begins to try to retrieve the money. Mother, hearing her husband scream, leaves the baby in the tub and rushes into the living quarters to try to help him save some of the money, which is quickly burning up in the fire.

At some point, the mother remembers she has left the baby in the tub, listens, can't hear the child, and rushes into the bathroom only to find that the baby has drowned. She screams, comes back into the living quarters with the dead baby in her arms, and the two parents grieve over the child. They have lost all.

Actors need all the help they can get to create the reality of that story! One false move and the play could become grotesquely untruthful. Many actors find it hard to believe in the circumstances of a play like this, and my partner and I had no idea how to give the scene truth. Our emotions just couldn't change that fast or that radically without some outside help.

By physically performing specific actions such as picking something up, trying to smell or feel the texture of an object, or simply running toward a place, you will conjure up memories and feelings. It also works, however, that when you create a certain feeling, you will act or behave in a particular way. For instance, if *you* think about something that makes you sad, you will do things that indicate you are sad.

There are two ways of acting that make use of these dynamics. One is Stanislavsky's method of conjuring up feelings and allowing these feelings to dictate the way you act in a scene. However, there is anouther school of acting where simply *doing* the action will automatically create the emotion. Your feelings will come up from whatever you have just physically performed. Either way will connect mind with body.

Chapter 16

The Private Moment Exercise

I Can Remember and Remember Well

The Private Moment Exercise comes naturally out of the "As If" Exercise. It is almost an extension of it. It is used to help you uncover your real identity, the one you probably feel you have always needed to hide in order to satisfy someone else. This exercise helps you resolve hiding behavior and allows you to delve deeper into secrecy and intimacy issues.

Abuse survivors often find that they have very little sense of an independent identity, so they often search wildly and frantically for any identity that they can adopt. They may constantly "borrow" ideas, fashion, convictions, and even plans from other people, whether or not these people are appropriate models. As you begin to create that which is truly yours, inside and out, you will find your own individual identity. The Private Moment Exercise is the next step in that quest.

When actors do this exercise in class, they use it to do something private and personal in front of others—something they wouldn't normally do in public because it would be too embarrassing and revealing. However, an inherent problem with this exercise for those in the performing arts is their overwhelming desire to be outrageous. In most beginning acting classes, there are always one or two actors who cannot resist the temptation to urinate, masturbate, or act out other reality moments that people do in private. These are not considered private moments.

A private moment is a moment of bonding with ourselves, touching on something we love about ourselves, but a moment that we may be too embarrassed to share with others. These are moments in which we seek to energize ourselves in flights of fantasy. We may find ourselves singing or dancing or doing other things we wished we could share with the public but until now felt too embarrassed or ashamed to admit we do. These are real private moments.

Have you ever sung off-tune in the shower, pretending to be a Broadway musical star—momentarily believing that your singing is even better than the real star? Well, that is a private moment. And it is the beginning of self-love and self-hope.

A private moment deepens the experience of understanding our embarrassment, shyness, and unavailability in relationships. During the abuse episodes, perpetrators may have been shaming, ridiculing, judging: all the elements of embarrassment and the need to escape in adulthood. The humiliation and self-doubt that occurred during and after the abuse incident or incidents are usually submerged in an unrealistic appraisal of what we can expect in life now. For instance, many survivors expect violent and physical confrontations in their adult relationships. Because of the disrespect we suffered, we feel we are not wanted by others now. That leads to feelings of isolation and being essentially alone, like the odd-person out. We were the ones that others whispered about in school, the kids who felt that we didn't belong anywhere. Your private moment will help you deal head on with your anger over these indignities.

Perhaps you never realized the depth and extent of the damage that was done to you by these insults. The Private Moment Exercise will be an aid for you to root out these feelings and rediscover how outside of the "inner sanctum" you felt, but now with a deeper understanding of why. Your abuse opened the door to a prison in which you've probably spent a good deal of time hiding, never feeling safe about who you were or what you wanted and needed, and feeling guilty that somehow you caused all this and it was your fault.

As you use the Private Moment Exercise to look squarely at what happened, you will find that you no longer need to forget. You will be able to see that how you reacted was a survival tactic; you will be able to stop blaming yourself for your failures in life and start believing that a fulfilled life can now become a reality. Now you will feel strong enough to identify false hopes and fanciful wishes. You will find yourself searching for your real strengths in life and begin to implement them to live more fully. Now you will be able to ask for what you want and need freely.

The Private Moment Exercise

1. In order for your private moment to no longer be private, you will need some kind of an audience. If you are not in a group or class where these exercises can be done, ask a friend or your therapist to be your audience and explain to them the purpose of the exercise.

2. Take the time to do a fifteen minute relaxation exercise using sunshine or another relaxing motif. Your audience will wait and it's important for you to begin to realize that your time and effort are as important as anyone else's.

3. When you feel ready, begin to create the environment in which the private moment will take place—the bathroom, the bedroom, the kitchen, the outdoors, a park, etc.

4. Create the atmosphere fully and carefully. Create the weather. If it is cool in your atmosphere, put on a sweater or some other indication that the temperature is a certain degree. Put objects in and around your environment that would have normally been there, such as a specific chair or table, trees, plants, water, animals—whatever you would expect to find there.

5. Now begin to walk around and feel yourself in this environment. Talk out loud: Where are you? Are you comfortable? Are the time and place you usually do this private moment exactly the way they usually are? Anything missing?

6. Begin to describe out loud what you're doing. Are you listening to music? Are you about to dance to this music? Are you going to sing? Jump on your bed? Talk to yourself? About what? Do you have an Academy Award speech you are working out?

7. Then begin to do what you usually secretly do in this environment. Let your audience hear your song or Academy Award speech.

8. Don't stop yourself by judging your performance or trying to see how your audience is responding. By being as specific and detail-oriented as possible, you will help yourself to concentrate fully on what you are creating. So you'll be less inclined to self-judge.

9. When you feel you have accomplished as much of the private moment as you can, stop, face your audience, and speak to them only in terms of feelings: I feel embarrassed; I feel relieved; I feel scared; I feel strong.

Some popular private moment exercises in acting class have been: dancing the flamenco to *Carmen*; extemporaneously making up poetry in front of the audience; making a speech in running for public office; or telling someone off in a verbal confrontation. My actor friend Richard got on the stage to do this exercise and found himself sitting in a chair brooding for half an hour. We in the audience waited impatiently for something to happen. All of a sudden, he jumped up and began viciously punching an imagined adversary while screaming epithets. When his energies were spent, he sat back down in the chair and went back to his brooding. At first, he was very ashamed that his inner anger had finally been revealed to others, until the coach reassured him that he had successfully completed expressing a valuable part of himself publicly. Now he would never be afraid of those hidden emotions again. In other words, he had made himself vulnerable on the stage and found that he was able to handle it. That is a paramount part of any actor's repertoire: being able to be private in public.

But embarrassment can be expressed differently for different people. Child abuse may result in some people developing shy and withdrawn personalities, while others become overly boisterous or act as the class clown. Still others may become defensively loud.

Overbearing personalities and/or extreme or seemingly abnormal personality styles often result from extreme emotional abuse. People with these personality types may be trying to fill up the void left inside from unloving and uncaring parents or guardians. They use their personalities as a way of proving to themselves and others that they really are nice, easygoing, and fun-loving people. They feel that if those emotions overshadow their real feelings of shame and doubt that perhaps the former feelings will be overridden, like writing over sentences on a computer. But, unfortunately, it doesn't work that way. Those hidden feelings of embarrassment, shame, and self-judgment just fester until they come out in righteous indignation, anger, or paranoid thinking that people are out to "get" you.

Some survivors fear that if their abusive histories are ever discovered by others, especially their love partners, the shame may end up threatening the relationship. One client of mine could not speak to anyone except for the most intimate of her immediate circle of friends because she was so afraid of being criticized and judged. You've probably heard others say, "If people really knew me, they'd hate me." This is the same sort of fear survivors feel, but to an even more "shameful" degree because of the secrecy shrouding child abuse.

By using the private moment, you will begin to create your own personality style to fit you; you will find a real self instead of living a false one. And you will be able to gain control over unnerving, disgusting, secretive, or shameful feelings so that your own self can come through.

Laura's Story

Laura was a quiet, small woman who had been confident and successful in front of other actors in acting school. She had been the first to volunteer to go up on the stage for improvisations and "sudden scenes" where she needed to learn lines quickly and then perform them that evening. Nothing seemed to phase her in class. However, once on the professional circuit, she found herself overly shy and afraid of auditioning. When she began working in front of casting directors, producers, and directors, she became terrified. Even a glass of vodka was not enough to help overcome feelings of being untalented and insecure when she did a "cold reading"—reading part of the script to show producers how she would perform a role. Instead, she would sit outside the casting office before her audition, downing half a bottle of booze just to get the courage to go in.

Laura told herself these drinks were just to help her overcome stage fright. And worse, she believed that no one could smell the liquor on her breath once she went into the room. As role after role was lost and she began to hear uncomplimentary things being said about her behind her back, Laura realized that her shyness, fears, and insecurities were apparent to everyone. She also realized that people knew she was hiding behind alcohol.

Laura's private moment was heart wrenching. It took weeks before the class and the coach could convince her to attempt one. Even now, as an adult actress, she felt terrified of revealing any of her childhood shame. It was just so difficult to keep her mind on what she was doing. She found herself constantly wanting to look out into the audience to see who was there and if they were laughing at her in ridicule.

Emotional abuse is confusing, usually consisting of contradictory demands by the perpetrator as a power source to make the victim feel inferior and subjugated. In adulthood, Laura continued the pattern of wanting a successful, happy career but denying herself one because she had been told that she was tarnished, that she would never be good enough, and that she especially could never be as good as her mother.

So in adulthood, Laura found that she only felt safe when it didn't matter; when she was supposed to be learning and mistakes were an expected part of her training. The minute she needed to put all that study and practice into a professional situation, she froze. She couldn't afford to be hurt the way she had been by her mother. She couldn't stand to be judged negatively; everyone had to like her, love her even. She couldn't bear to be less than perfect. Memories of her mother demanding that everything she did be perfect came flooding back during her Private Moment Exercise.

During her private moment, a dance commemorating spring, Laura remembered sitting on her bed envisioning a spring dance she had once seen a soloist perform in a professional dance company. Laura tried to emulate the dancer in the privacy of her bedroom, when her mother suddenly and unexpectedly opened the bedroom door, stood in the doorway, and watched Laura do a particularly difficult contortion. When Laura saw her mother watching, she immediately stopped. But with the little she had seen, the mother felt free to criticize Laura's performance. When Laura objected, her mother replied, "If I criticize you too much, it's only because I want you to be perfect!" Once this memory emerged, Laura also remembered how her mother never thought she was pretty enough, slim enough, or smart enough. Memories began to flood in of being compared to other girls the family knew. Some of these people were not even close to Laura or her mother; it would have been impossible to know if the girls were all that they'd been given credit for being.

Once it became clear to Laura that her verbal and emotional abuse at home had contributed to low self-esteem and hatred of herself as well as her failure to succeed as an actress, she began to use the Private Moment Exercise to create a strong ego, one where she could feel "just as good as anyone else who was auditioning." She did not have to be the best—she simply had to do the best she could at that moment.

Once the burden of having to be perfect left her, she became a successful series star. She has enjoyed her acting immensely and finds that she does not make unreasonable expectations of her own children.

After the exercise, Laura sat on the side of the stage, faced the other students, and debriefed the exercise with us. Laura reported that she had felt humiliated that those were her private thoughts: that her mother's was an abuser who used Laura to act out her own fantasies of having the most perfect daughter in the world.

Because the Private Moment Exercise had brought up a particular time in Laura's life, she was able to remember that she had often had fantasies as a child about pleasing her father, too. The only time he treated her well occurred when she transformed herself into someone else for him. Then he appeared to accept her, didn't blindly agree with her mother in ridiculing her, and perhaps even loved her for that moment. Fantasies of how she could have been more for her father, of never feeling she was good enough, consumed her waking life and prevented her from giving 100 percent to her acting career. By revealing her secret wishes to a supportive group, she was able to neutralize the shame and humiliation she had felt at being judged. Plus, her self-esteem was greatly boosted when she heard our applause for allowing us into her secret world. She had finally been really accepted by her peers and friends.

Being emotionally naked on stage is a primary requirement for actors. Honesty and the ability to allow the real self to emerge is also a requirement for love relationships in real life. A private moment is a great help in allowing you to explore your secret world, normalize it, and see that it isn't as embarrassing and shameful as you may have expected.

If you do the Private Moment Exercise in a therapy office, you may have to mimic or imaginarily create props or activities that are difficult to recreate in that environment. But remember, the more Private Moment exercises you do, the more details about your abuse and your childhood in general will come to you. Speak out loud about fears you feel others see. Remember, the Private Moment Exercise will be an aid in helping you discover your hidden emotions about your abuse and how you can change those patterns now, as an adult. The sooner you bring the memories and connecting emotions to consciousness, the sooner you will no longer be afraid of them, and the sooner you will neutralize them and integrate them into your personality. Then you will let go of them and move on.

Chapter 17

The Animal Exercise

I Can Be Whoever I Want to Be

The Animal Exercise is more of a transition from the environmental aspects of the external exercises to the internal exercises and to internal feeling states. So many times, abuse survivors, especially sexual abuse survivors, experience feelings of depersonalization and greatly restricted emotion—often for fear of losing control—and find themselves depressed. The Animal Exercise is a unique way to understand these emotions.

The idea of the Animal Exercise is that through imitating an animal, you become that beast. That creation will allow you to use your sensory imagination to the fullest to investigate how a species outside yourself might see, feel, taste, hear, and touch. As an animal, you will not be concentrating on particularly emotional events; you will be sidestepping jumping into the abuse. Instead, you will investigate your thoughts, feelings, or activities and will find that they are associated with your trauma, and your inability to remember all or some aspects of the trauma will be alleviated.

The Animal Exercise can be very personal and is better done alone until any embarrassment or humiliation is contained. This exercise usually gets gales of laughter in acting classes because people find the weirdest animals to emulate. I can remember acting class excursions to the Los Angeles Zoo where each student went from cage to cage trying to find an animal whose characteristics exemplified the character they needed to create.

The zoo is a favorite hangout for actors. Not only does the Animal Exercise compel an actor to create the nuances of a character, but it also helps him explore the character's "sense of being" (also called temperament) and idiosyncrasies in the world.

And as you look at all the different aspects of the animal including its movements and personality, you will discover what the animal might be thinking or feeling at any given moment. This is an important exercise in allowing your imagination to soar freely.

For sexual and physical abuse survivors, the Animal Exercise allows the opportunity of revealing secrets through the animal you create. Because you are not directly revealing your own secrets, but are using the animal to communicate through, you will be able to temper negative emotions brought up by your trauma. This exercise offers you the added benefit of not speaking prematurely about your life to others before you have had the opportunity to build up the strength to process what happened to you.

Undoubtedly, as a survivor you were held to secrecy, especially about your abuse issues. Now you can investigate all sides of another being while hiding nothing. You will not have to feel secretive or fearful because animals are free and guiless; they don't care that you watch them. They are uninhibited, unashamed, enthusiastic, and exploring—the way you once were. They are not embarrassed by what they do; but they are shamed when they are punished.

As you connect with their unabashed, moment-to-moment activity, you may connect with the freedom you want to recover. Obviously you are not going to be like an animal in life, but you are going to investigate the immediacy of their lives: the way they take life in the present.

The Animal Exercise

1. In this exercise you will choose an animal, any animal you wish, from a domestic dog or cat to something exotic that you see in a zoo, and you will become that animal by taking on its pose and beginning to act the way the animal acts.

2. Watch your dog or cat or go to the zoo and find an animal, bird, salamander, or other beast that interests you. Find an animal that "talks to you," one with whom you feel a symbiosis. Pick a specific animal and investigate how it moves within that world and the particular way it interacts with its environment. That way you will begin to see how specific and concentrated you can become in checking out *your* environment.

3. Watch the way that animal moves. Ask yourself, "How does the animal walk?" "Does it look at me?" "Is it a four-legged or two-legged creature?" "How does it become involved in its environment?" "Does it sniff, scratch, or move its head from side to side like a bear to investigate its environment?"

4. Take the physical stance of your animal. Investigate its movements. Take on those movements and begin to become involved in your immediate environment the way your animal would.

5. What do you see or hear as the animal? Are there special sounds you suspect you (as a human) would not hear that your animal might? What do you see as the animal? Are you an animal who can see in color? Not in color? Is your animal far-sighted, near-sighted, or seeing normally?

6. Begin to walk around your environment the way the animal would. Are you crawling, running, sprinting? Do you have jerky movements or are you smooth like a cat? What are you choosing to pick up in the environment? What piques your curiosity?

If you have chosen a monkey, you will probably be involved in seeing rather than smelling. There will be a lot of picking up curious things off the floor and jumping around. If you have chosen a cat, there will be stealth-like movement, a slowness often followed by a fast retreat. Does the cat have a coy demeanor with suspicious glances at people to see what they are going to do next?

If you are creating a dog, be sure you pick a particular breed of dog. If you have chosen a boxer, you will find a beast that is drooling, gazing, and quick to investigate its environment, and the movements will be jerky and probably uncoordinated. If your animal is an Airedale terrier, like mine, the movements will be sudden and the animal will undoubtedly be in constant motion, watching everything in its environment in order to pounce! If it is a Saint Bernard, the movements might be slower and sleepier.

The Animal Exercise is a freeing exercise. Once you have created a few animals and investigated your environment using yourself as the animal you created, you will feel empowered to use your real self to investigate your own environment.

Go to your pad of paper and write down on a separate page all the feelings and memories that have come up for you while doing this exercise.

Chapter 18

The Gibberish Exercise

Communication at All Costs

Adult abuse survivors often are unable to talk about or describe what happened during and after their abuse. Their inability to speak out about their pain, because of feelings of shame, is one of the most critical problems in overcoming the aftereffects of any kind of child abuse. It can be especially difficult to express the pain and anger or even describe the memories of what happened to you if the abuse occurred preverbally (usually the time from your birth to about two years old), before you were able to actually speak words in understandable sentences.

Gibberish consists of spontaneously made-up sounds—nonsense words that have no meaning themselves. The Gibberish Exercise can be considered a bridge between speech and nonsense syllables that are the same types of sounds that little children utter just before they are able to speak words, when you were just learning to talk. Except now you're going to go back to those sounds to express feelings you may have but are unable to talk about.

The Gibberish Exercise was created to help actors become more real in their characters. Many new actors do their best to memorize their lines and then pray that they won't forget them during filming or during a stage performance. For them, the essence of the scene is forgotten because of their fear of forgetting dialogue. The Gibberish Exercise was originally designed to help these actors get away from mouthing their lines. It was an aid in helping them find nonverbal ways of completing an action or objective—it allowed them to really involve themselves in the situation of a scene so that their dialogue could flow naturally from what they were trying to accomplish.

More seasoned actors know that simply saying dialogue without any meaning behind the words will lead to mechanical acting. In this kind of acting, no real thought process lies behind the lines the actor is saying. In order to overcome this problem, coaches often use the Gibberish Exercise.

In the Gibberish Exercise, actors are not allowed to use language as we know it. They cannot even speak in their native tongue. Instead, they use gibberish sounds that are made up in the moment. An example would be, "Geebul ger ah fo" or any indiscernible, out-loud uttering. The coach then gives the actor a task or an objective to accomplish without using real words, but using only these made-up sounds.

A variation on the Gibberish Exercise is pretending to speak in a foreign language. That can have the same effect of speaking nonsense syllables—only feelings and the desire to express emotion count here. The Gibberish Exercise helps actors work spontaneously, using moment-to-moment reactions. They become very aware of the character's immediate environment, so that they are no longer hung up on words.

When actors cannot use formal language, they often describe their bodies as feeling more alive than ever, and the mind/body connection seems more complete. Intuitions may seem even more acute and on target. The Gibberish Exercise forces you to act honestly, with meaning behind every gesture.

A dramatic example might be trying to prevent someone from going too near the train tracks when a train is coming into a station. Given the immediacy of helping that person not step in front of the train and get run over, the actor is literally forced by the exercise to accomplish saving that person's life by the intensity with which the gibberish is spoken. Hand and eye movements combined with other bodily expressions all help indicate the imminent danger without real words.

What purpose will these results serve for abuse survivors? Well, survivors can use this exercise to help themselves segue from nonverbal expression about their abuse into ultimately feeling strong enough to use words to describe it. As you tell your story in gibberish, you will begin to train yourself to speak in real language.

Remember, in gibberish no one else really knows what you're saying—only *you* know. That is the first step in revelation. As you become more and more comfortable in "telling" your story in sounds without words, you may find that when you finally decide you can reveal your abuse experience in English, it won't be so difficult. You have trained yourself to begin the revealing process. You may even find yourself relieved that you are now able to let those secrets out that you have kept hidden for so long. This exercise is useful in helping you overcome your embarrassment, humiliation, shame, or inability to reveal yourself, your past, or your abuse.

For child abuse survivors, the Gibberish Exercise can also help define the meaning of the abuse; the feelings that came from it can be expressed without words.

The Gibberish Exercise can be a tool that works as an entrée into finding the ability to tell your story in words. As you reveal what happened in gibberish, you may feel you are already breaking the secrecy and realize that you have begun to share your story.

The Gibberish Exercise

1. Give yourself an objective that is very action-oriented, such as warning someone about an immediate danger, convincing someone to buy something, or begging someone to do something for you. It might feel like charades. Begin to warn, sell, or entice the other person using gibberish—do not use any real words. You can pretend to speak in a foreign language if that sounds more interesting.

2. Ideally, you will use a real, live human being to work with (a trusted friend, a partner, or a member of a therapy group). But if you're working on these exercises alone, you might pretend to use the telephone or create an imaginary person to talk to, or you can simply imagine a person to talk to.

3. Create the props in your environment you will need in order to succeed in convincing, warning, or begging the other person to do what you need them to do.

4. Really look at the other person. Or, if you are on the phone, listen closely to their voice on the other end of the line. Do you think they understand what you are trying to convey? How do you know whether or not they "get it"? Perhaps you can tell by their sense of being, their look, or their tone of voice in response to you.

5. If you are convinced that they don't understand what you are trying to tell them, what else can you use to get it across to them? Pictures, photos, hand movements, the inflection of your voice, your affect, your enthusiasm, eye contact, or careful mimicry of the situation can be very convincing and forceful. Be very definite in what you want to convey and continue discovering new ways of sending the message without real language.

6. Stop. Have you accomplished what you set out to do? Do you think the other person understands the meaning behind your gibberish words? How do you know? What tells you that you have succeeded in your endeavor?

7. Go to your pad of paper and write down the feelings, frustrations, and concerns that have come up in the exercise.

Chapter 19

The Telephone Exercise

The Transitional Object

The natural extension of the Gibberish Exercise is to connect with others verbally and begin the process of telling your story to someone else, even if that person is imaginary. The next two exercises are used expressly for overcoming your isolation and perhaps even alienation from other people. Remember that revealing your story to a sympathetic person helps you begin to integrate the feelings you still have about it. As a mature, adult person, you can now realize that by telling your story, you will discover more about what affects it has for you in your current life. Connections with the way you act in your life now to the aftereffects of your abuse will become obvious. Once you pinpoint exactly how the abuse still controls you, you will find that you can dump those ways of being in the world that do not serve you and find new and more adaptive solutions.

But it is hard to trust other people when your own family has been unsupportive, disbelieving, or outright abusive. The main point of the next two exercises is to help you reach out to someone, first from your imagination, and then in person. You will begin to trust that your imagination, coming from your unconscious mind, will automatically bring to consciousness someone whom you really want to talk to. Many times abuse survivors find themselves talking to their abusers. But I ask that you take small steps at first.

You might ask yourself, "Whom do I really trust with the information I want to impart?" That will help you begin these exercises. Ultimately, you will be able to "speak" to your abuser.

Confrontation is one of the things that scares abuse survivors the most. The anticipation of ever talking to or being in the presence of the abuser again can cause abuse survivors to wonder, "What would I say? How would I act? I want to tell him/her off, but I know I would be cotton-mouthed."

Like other forms of communication, confrontation must be approached slowly, very much like creeping up on something. The Telephone Exercise has a unique format and is the perfect exercise for breaking that silence and beginning to experience confronting the abuser. In this exercise, the telephone receiver, disconnected from the phone, is used to "listen" for the voice of whomever you need to talk to on the other end. Sometimes it is the abuser, and the telephone acts as a buffer between you and that person.

Again, because you are creating all aspects of this exercise yourself, you are also in control of all the implements: the telephone, the receiver, and the voice on the other end. You are also in control of how that phone call progresses. For abuse survivors, this can be the first time confronting the abuser with strength and determination instead of fear and dread.

Annie's Story

After five years in group therapy, Annie was finally able to confront her abuser, an older brother who had bullied her and frightened her during most of her childhood. The Telephone Exercise was her breakthrough exercise because up to that time she could only cry and give details about her abuse. She felt helpless to act on her feelings in an appropriate yet forceful way. After the Telephone Exercise, Annie found the words she wanted to say and the bravery she had up to now lacked. The Telephone Exercise had offered her the forum to prioritize what she needed to say, and the language with which she needed to say it.

The Telephone Exercise

1. Unplug the receiver from your phone or, if it's a mobile phone, make sure it's turned off (you don't want a *real* phone call interrupting your exercise!). Pull a chair up to a table and place the phone receiver on the table, while you sit in the chair.

2. As you look at the phone or receiver, repeat the words, "I anticipate nothing. I anticipate nothing."

3. Now, pick up the receiver and put it to your ear. Just listen. Trust your unconscious to bring to mind the person you really want to talk to. At first you may not hear anyone. In that case, put the receiver down and pick it up again, fresh. Put it to your ear and listen very carefully. See who comes into your mind. That is the person with whom you wish to speak.

4. As you listen to their "voice," say the first word that comes to mind, no matter how out of context you may think that word may be. As you say the word and continue to listen, see if a response is forthcoming from the other person. If you "hear" an answer, respond to what they say to you.

If you cannot imagine a response from the phantom person on the other end of the phone, say another word; then say a sentence.

5. A flood of images will probably come forward. Images might include how the person on the other end of the line might look and how they might verbally respond. You probably knew this person (or know them now) better than you ever realized by doing this exercise. Experience these images, and respond out loud to them.

6. When you finish your conversation, either say goodbye or simple hang up.

7. Write down or tape-record your feelings. With whom were you speaking? What happened? What do you think made you deal with that person at this time?

The Telephone Exercise allows you to use your imagination directly—by picking up a receiver and imagining who is on the other end of the phone. Your imagination does all the work. Whomever's voice you need to "hear" on the other end of the phone will automatically come to you. Once you receive that voice in your mind, you will be able to respond now, as an adult, the way you need to in order to repair the hurt and pain done to you. The voice might be the abuser or it might be the parent who stood by and did nothing. Whoever comes forward, you will now be starting to rehearse by speaking into an unplugged receiver what you will ultimately end up saying to that person for real.

Each time you complete the Telephone Exercise, the voice of a person on the other end will come in clearer and clearer. Often different people will present themselves, and an entire scenario of the time you need to remember will unfold. Again, use your judgment as to how deeply you wish to pursue your memories.

Chapter 20

The Academy Award Speech Exercise

What do you want in your life? What will make you feel successful and complete now and in the future? That may seem like an inordinately difficult question until you take a look at all the people around you now who have been a part of your life and who opened doors for you or encouraged you to take opportunities.

No, that doesn't mean you are a "user" or that you are just looking for people who can "do" something for you. Not at all. But it does mean that part of helping yourself to overcome your past and the aftereffects stemming from it is finding people in your life who are *good* for you—people who understand you and who are tolerant of you and your foibles. These people will hopefully know when to come forward toward you and be a part of your life and when to recede, giving you space and time to work out your problems, allowing you to come back to them when you feel like it.

The Academy Award Speech Exercise is very popular with actors of all ages. In fact, I simply do not know of an actor, no matter how early he or she is in his or her career, who has not devised the best Academy Award speech in the world for when (certainly not *if*) he or she wins that coveted trophy. Long, drawn out thank-yous go to everyone from a current spouse to a first-grade teacher. Reminiscence of how particular people helped the actor to develop as an artist and a person are emotionally delivered.

But for abuse survivors, the Academy Award Speech Exercise has an even more special meaning. When you give your speech, probably in front of a mirror or in the shower, you will notice all the people who come to mind in your life past and present who were, and are, on your side.

As you hold your "award" and give thanks, you may notice that there are people right now who are not only there for you, but who want to be a part of your life now. They hold the key to how you can use your newfound freedom from abuse to push yourself forward in your life. Notice who comes to mind as you give the speech. Don't force people to come to mind—just let your unconscious do the work.

You may find the abuser coming to mind as the "anti-helper." Because this is *your* speech and not in front of the Academy of Motion Picture Arts and Sciences, speak out loud about how you were held back by that person. Then, as quickly as you can, go back to those who come to mind who are here now, and who can move you forward in your life.

Again, because you are working with pushing unwanted people out of your consciousness when the unconscious brings them forward and keeping well-wishers and positive people *in* your consciousness when they emerge, you are exercising your ability to control. Isn't that what you've been looking for all along?

The Academy Award Speech Exercise

1. Relax and empty your mind. You can be anywhere when you do this exercise, but it is preferable that you stand while giving your speech.
2. Pick up an object that could stand in for your Academy Award.
3. Create the "fourth wall" in your imagination and put people out there all looking at you. You have just won the Academy Award. If you are a stickler for detail, you might tell yourself what you won it for—acting, directing, producing, editing, etc.
4. Look out at the audience as you hold your award. Do you see any familiar faces out there? Whose?
5. Now look at the award. Is it bright, dull, heavier than you anticipated, lighter? Is it smooth, or are there ridges? Is it cool in your hand or warm?
6. Now begin to speak out loud. Just tell the "audience" in front of you how grateful you are for the award. Or, perhaps you are like one of those actors who scorns any award and despises comparisons with other performers. Fine, go with that. But remember, we want a positive, forward-moving and action-oriented thank-you so that you can recognize and acknowledge all the good people in your life right now.

   Remember, too, that we are looking for your unconscious mind to come forward. If you push yourself to remember particular people or force memories in any way, you will be defeating the purpose of the exercise, which is to find out what is really and truly on your unconscious mind right now. That is the "curative" factor. Once you uncover who you are really thinking about and the relationship you have with that person, you will put yourself in the reality of this moment and know how to proceed to get what you want now.

7. Now, out loud, ask yourself, "Who was the most positive person in my life up to now?" Allow the memory of that person to come forward and begin to thank him or her. Just say the first things that come out of your mouth—don't edit yourself. Because you are doing this exercise alone, in the privacy of your own home, you can say whatever you need to. If you wish to change what you just said, change it. The point is to allow the unconscious to come forward. You may be very surprised to see whom you remember!

8. Now ask yourself, "Who is the person in my life right now that seems to be on my side? What tells me that that person is for me?" Speak out loud and thank that person for whatever they have contributed to your life right now.

9. Continue to speak out loud, thanking whomever comes to mind.

10. The speech can be as long or as short as you need it to be. Remember, when you do these exercises again later, new people will come to mind to be thanked.

11. Write on your pad or speak into your tape recorder all the feelings and memories you can from this exercise. What particularly stood out for you as you thanked the people who deserved to be recognized in your life. Were you happy for the opportunity to finally feature them as a good part of your life, remember them, and identify how they were or are a help in your emotional, physical being, or in your work right now? If no one comes to mind, consider who you know in your life right now who could become a mentor or friend to you. Remember, this speech is an exploration for who can be a positive force in your life.

This exercise is a nice sequel into the Preparation-Before-a-Scene Exercise. It will help you remember what atmosphere, objects, and environment you need to create in order to deal with people in your life. And, best of all, it will allow you to create the groundwork and foundation for your relationships to unfold so that you feel a part of others' lives and know where you fit in with those people around you.

Chapter 21

The Inner Monologue Exercise

I Can Convince Myself, Talk Myself Out of It, or Problem Solve

The Inner Monologue Exercise differs from the Academy Award Exercise in that it is an inner monologue rather than a dialogue. A monologue is used in acting to help the character figure out a problem outside or inside himself, to give him courage to do some dangerous feat, or to help him reminisce—an escape into reverie or fantasy to help him discover what he wishes he could do in reality. Sometimes it is an inner pep talk. It can work the same way for abuse survivors.

All kinds of abuse—sexual, physical, emotional, and verbal—strip us of our ability to talk out; to speak out about our needs and wants. Our true feelings become so hidden that they are all but forgotten. Like a muscle that is never exercised and becomes weak and useless, our "selves" are lost. The Inner Monologue Exercise is by far my favorite exercise because it is a stream-of-consciousness discourse that allows you to begin to speak your inner thoughts without any prior thought at all. Because the words are thoughts about anything and everything, or a particular situation, this exercise can be the closest finder of the truth I know. To make it simple: it is simply about what you are thinking. But not just what you're thinking randomly. The Inner Monologue helps wandering thoughts suddenly become directed to a particular event, place, situation, or commentary.

"In vino veritas" goes the old adage—"In wine there is truth." I find that the most truth lies in the Inner Monologue. Because whatever you are thinking spontaneously is probably what is in your unconscious mind, and speaking it may even trigger bringing the unconscious to consciousness, which is the main purpose of psychotherapy.

This exercise also acts as a rehearsal for when you decide how you want to break your secrecy. It helps you talk yourself out of shame and recrimination, and aids you in establishing how you want to make healthy personal and sexual contacts. Just like an actor uses inner monologues as the character in order to convince herself, solve a problem, or rationalize an action, you can use inner monologues as an abuse survivor to talk to yourself about the options, possibilities, and inner strengths you have in order to accomplish whatever you need to do to recover. The Inner Monologue is similar to a soliloquy in Shakespeare.

The Inner Monologue Exercise

1. Give yourself a problem to solve, like whether you should confront someone about a conflict you have with them. This might entail a problem you are currently having with a friend or a coworker.

2. Speak out loud—whatever comes to mind about the problem. Has someone at work tried to steal your job? Has a boyfriend borrowed money he has not returned? How do you want to deal with those problems? Begin to problem solve out loud. You will be amazed at how you think, what annoys you, what you truly find funny, interesting, and telling.

3. Don't plan your monologue, just let it evolve out of your mouth. Whatever comes to mind, verbalize.

4. As you continue to speak from your unconscious mind, you will begin to notice a pattern forming: The mind forces sentences and phrases to make sense. What you really need to hear, you will automatically think or say.

5. Now begin to work harder at the task you have undertaken.

6. Notice the emotional pattern that forms out of your monologue. Is it angry, sad, forceful, stimulating, positive?

7. This exercise can work especially well when you have an accompanying physical task, such as untangling a telephone cord or trying to get a key off of your keychain. Try to work out the problem while doing an unrelated task. You'll be surprised what comes out verbally.

An Example

The soundman who worked on a play I was in was trying his hardest to bind two wires together to give a stereophonic sound to a particular piece of music. The equipment was old (as is true of most theater machines in small theaters) and he couldn't get the effect he wanted. As he began to talk to himself out loud, the chatter became more about his impending divorce from a well-known actress than it was about the equipment.

The machine he was using was actually *becoming* his estranged wife as he pushed it, prodded it, and tried to get it to do what he needed it to do. Phrases such as "You selfish pig" and "Why won't you ever do what I need you to do?" were emerging fast and furious, until he realized that others were watching and listening!

The Inner Monologue Exercise allowed Cathy to explore how she would tell her father how she felt about his treatment of her in childhood. It acted as a tool for her to convince herself that she could confront him, and that she had been short-changed by the shabby, inconsiderate and, disrespectful treatment her father had given her.

By the time she had finished the exercises, she had mustered up enough strength and conviction in herself that when she finally confronted her father, she was ready! She knew exactly where she wanted to begin the encounter: in a café in the Chinatown area of San Francisco. And she knew exactly how she wanted to open the conversation: with an example to him of how much she had needed him to be on her side as a child, how humiliated she had been when he left the family, and what she wanted from her father now: an apology and an understanding of how she had suffered. She demanded that he tell her how he imagined her childhood must have been, just so she could see if he truly understood.

Cathy had been vindicated and she wanted to move on with her life and explore the love and understanding she felt she could now give.

Chapter 22

The Dying Exercise

Life Is Worth Living

The Dying Exercise is really an exercise in rebirth. Fear of success, fear of loving, fear of relationships, fear of friendships, and fear of trusting all seem to fade when you realize that life is finite. What would your last wishes be? What did you not do in this life that you really wanted to do? The Dying Exercise helps you look at these questions and reminds you of what you have always wanted to accomplish in your life.

As I said, the idea of "dying" as an exercise is to help you really bring yourself to life: to rebirth yourself. Instead of imagining suicide or self-mutilating behavior as a way of calling for help from others, the Dying Exercise will be an aid for you to call on help from yourself. Thus, you empower yourself. You don't have to depend on fate or someone else or wait for something to happen so that you can live your life fully and successfully. As you work this exercise, you will find that your focus is on internal mental and physical processes of your body during the last physical thing you will ever do in this world—die.

For abuse survivors, a serious note may emerge. Survivors often describe that their innocence and safety were "killed off" by the abuse. And, in a way, they are right. Their ability to trust may have seemed forever lost, too. But discovering that you can use your own power to become reborn again can bring new life and strong hope into your body and spirit.

Many actors love dying in movies and on the stage because it is so dramatic and calls for all their emotions to come forward in a last gasp of life. I did a television series one year in which one of the costars took an inordinate time dying. He coughed and sputtered and lay there, looking far away and terribly mortal.

Then he suddenly became lucid again before finally falling back and expiring altogether. His dying moment took so long that it had to be edited down!

For abuse survivors, the Dying Exercise should not be a freaky, frightening affair. You are not meant to scare yourself so much that you become revictimized. It is actually an exercise of self-control. If you can make yourself die, you most certainly can make yourself live. This exercise is just another tool meant to help you find out how you want to change your life right now and what you will ultimately find satisfying. The exercise is also useful for turning anger into action—preparing for a confrontation and affirming your progress as you strive for success.

The Dying Exercise

1. Find a place where you can sprawl out—the floor, a bed, a couch—or slump down in a chair.

2. Give yourself a reason for your death—someone has mortally wounded you, you are dying of consumption (TB), or you are old and are ready to go. Make this reason something that hasn't come close to you in real life. Avoid choosing any brush with death experienced by you or someone close to you. Otherwise, you might frighten yourself out of the exercise.

3. Make your method of dying specific so that you can experience it from the inside out.

4. Take your dying position and begin to ask questions such as, "Can I breathe?" "What is my breathing like?" "Am I scared or am I resigned?" "Do I feel pain anywhere?" "What do I remember, or what am I thinking about?" "Am I looking inward now rather than outward?" "Do I have a sense of spirituality?"

5. Now begin to "die." Breathe more shallowly, attempt to take the next breath. Feel your energy seeping out of you. As you "die," do you see the next world? What do you see?

6. After you have "died," bring yourself back to life. Find a reason to live: your career, romantic partner, love, children, people who need to hear your story to help them through life. This will enable you to breathe life back into yourself. What is the first thing you think about? Is it something like, "Where am I?" or "What century is this?"

7. Now open your eyes. If they were open when you "died," bring yourself to consciousness and begin to breathe regularly. Look around and rediscover your surroundings. What is the first thing you see? Can you make it out? What colors do you see? What objects or shapes?

8. Are there any people around? Who? Are they speaking to you? What is your first wish? To get up off the ground or off the couch?

9. Now take a few more breaths and then go to your pad of paper and write down as many of your feelings as you can. Remember all the reasons you have for living, and describe how your life has changed since the abuse. How much further can you change it now that you are aware of how you want to live? How has the abuse has affected you, and how will you manage those aftereffects?

Perhaps the greatest contribution of the Dying Exercise is the fact that it helps focus on what was "killed." Many clients tell me that during this exercise all kinds of thoughts come up, thoughts they never realized they had: What have I done with my life? How am I living it right now? What is in the way of my happiness and contentment? Where do I go from here?

If the Dying Exercise is too realistic at first, my advice is to keep your "third eye" open, and if you start to feel overwhelmed, stop and write down the feelings that have come up so far. Then do another Sunshine (Relaxation) Exercise. The Dying Exercise can be tried again another time when you're feeling stronger.

After you have successfully worked the Dying Exercise, you will probably be reminded that you not only want to put a stop to wandering purposelessly in life, being limited and cramped by your past, but that now you have an important future, one you are in the process of creating in this moment.

Lil's Story

Lil felt she had no life. She had attempted suicide three times by overdosing on depression medication. Now her doctor had insisted that her husband give her the pills as they were prescribed and not allow her near the bottle unsupervised.

When Lil came to therapy, her thinking bordered on the psychotic. She sought therapy because she was having out-of-body experiences and abuse flashbacks. She had trouble sleeping because she was afraid someone would sneak into the house and kill her. At one point, she thought her husband was trying to poison her with her depression medication when he offered her one pill—the prescribed amount.

Lil was even too frightened to come to therapy by herself. She thought the therapist would call the police and she would be involuntarily confined for an indeterminate amount of time in a mental institution. Her husband accompanied her to our first session. He did all the talking as Lil stared vacantly at the floor, barely able to say hello to me.

Lil had also acquired an eating disorder. As she got thinner and thinner, she reported becoming more and more fearful of physical force. She described a childhood filled with bullying. When I met her that first time she was so shy I remember wondering how she had ever managed to date enough to finally get married.

Lil was truly helpless. The messages her father had given to her from the time she could remember were: "You're powerless," "You're not worthy of love or even recognition as a person." These messages froze Lil to such an extent that she couldn't even have a checkbook because she didn't know how to keep an account; she couldn't bring up her children, she couldn't shop alone, and her husband did all the cooking. She needed extra sleep during the day because she couldn't sleep at night. She kept over twenty-five bottles of pills of all kinds by her bedside; when she awoke in the morning they were the first things she took so that she wouldn't have anxiety attacks.

Lil began the exercises after six months of barely talking in therapy. She agreed to start them if her husband and I worked them with her. Her execution of the Coffee Cup Exercise was the first time I saw Lil laugh. She used the Shower Exercise as her private moment because she was so shy about her body. Her school mates had chided her about being so thin that she couldn't even pretend to be undressed in a shower in front of her husband and me without hiding behind a drapery in my office, pretending it were a shower curtain. Then she called out her emotions, feelings, and memories to us, secure that we could not see her. Later, she was actually able to do the Shower Exercise in her own bedroom and used it again as a private moment revelation. Finally, the Dying Exercise was accomplished by Lil's dying in her husband's arms. But during that exercise, a strange thing happened—she began laughing. She started telling her husband how angry she was that she hadn't been able to "beat up my former husband." As she began to "live" again, she transformed. She sat straight up in the chair and announced how things would be different. In fact, she was suddenly assertive enough to ask that I reduce my fee because she felt her husband was having too much trouble paying it!

Her confidence became more and more apparent as she confronted all the events in her life that seemed unfair. The Dying Exercise was truly transforming. It helped her segue into the next exercise, the Preparation-Before-a-Scene, which ultimately allowed her to confront her father in a therapeutic and positive way. The Dying Exercise seemed to help Lil free herself enough that a realization of how she wanted to raise her children came up: she had wanted input into their lives, and she had never had that. Her children were grown, so now perhaps she could have input into her grandchildren's lives.

Her rebirth allowed her to redirect her fears to where they belonged—in the past with the unpredictability of her family. Armed with that realization, she was finally able to take care of herself effectively in the present. Lil found that because of the Dying Exercise, her life was to revolve around children. She also began to set new goals, ones she could accomplish. She began a new career helping disturbed teens in a residential home. She reported that she wanted to protect them the way she had never been protected.

Chapter 23

The Affective Memory Exercise

I Remember Well

The last two exercises are called the Affective Memory Exercise and the Preparation-Before-a-Scene Exercise. One, the Affective Memory, deals with all the memories and feelings about your actual abuse situation. The other, the Preparation-Before-a-Scene, deals with preparing you to confront your abuser, whether he or she is alive or dead.

But remember, you are not trying to recreate the exact situation of your abuse in order to feel all the pain and fear you once had. Rather, you will be recreating the experience to capture all those emotions, gain control over them, begin to dissipate them, and start integrating them with who you are now. That is the beginning of knowing how to overcome the trauma in order to create and experience a mature, loving relationship without unwanted memories of abuse interfering.

Do not attempt to do the Affective Memory Exercise unless you feel you have successfully completed all of the exercises before it. This exercise will use every component of the preceding ones and really utilizes your sensory abilities. Initially, I recommend doing the exercise only in front of a carefully selected friend, a group, a therapist, or an acting coach just for the support they can provide. After doing the exercise a few times, though, you will be able to do it alone. Actors do it privately all the time as preparation for a very emotional scene. If you do decide to use a friend, tell him or her what you need them to do, which will be to guide you through your experience while you speak out sensorially about it. Then ask that person to help you deal with all the feelings that come up from the exercise.

The Affective Memory Exercise has three requirements:

1. *The Emotions:* The situation you will create must be very emotionally laden, and very traumatic, such as the abuse event. In fact, the main reason that this is the second to last emotional exercise of the Internal Exercises is that you will use it to sensorially recreate your abuse situation. But be careful. Although the exercise can be powerful, you will know when you feel ready because you have been rehearsing your control over strong emotional material in all the previous exercises. Remember to be careful and go only as far as feels right.

2. *The Sensations:* You can use the original abuse or any subsequent trauma for this exercise. But the point is that you use an extraordinary and meaningful incident. With the Affective Memory Exercise, you must make a decision: Do you feel comfortable recreating the abuse event sensorially, where you will reexperience the sensations and emotions you felt then? Or would you feel more comfortable simply speaking out loud and simply telling yourself the story of your abuse while at the same time describing the emotions and feelings connected with it as they come up? Either way will give you the same result: the ability to fill up gaps in your memory and incorporate the feelings you felt then into your adult personality now.

3. *The Seven-Year Rule:* Whatever trauma you decide to use must have occurred at least seven years ago. The thinking behind this is that it takes about seven years for you to adjust to the aftereffects and feelings of an ordeal. If you try to recreate the shock before seven years have passed, the memories may be way too sharp and you may become overwhelmed. However, after seven years, the feelings tend to blend into the personality, and you are more able to look at and deal with whatever happened.

Another thought behind the Affective Memory Exercise is that by age thirteen a person has experienced all the emotions known to humans—love, hate, fear, worry, sorrow, happiness, etc. Your emotions are no longer disconnected states; they have all melded into what is now your personality. That's why the event you recreate must be so dramatic and life altering: so that you can experience what these agitated responses feel like *now*.

One acting teacher I had warned actors that once they became adept at creating an Affective Memory Exercise, even after a hundred performances of a production, when that scene came where they needed to use their affective memory, the emotions would be just as strong and intense as they were the first time. In other words, an actor's emotions will be as powerful as the situation that initially prompted them.

For abuse survivors, however, the old feelings that will be brought up have been brought up for a reason: for you to transform them into more adaptive ways of thinking and behaving. You may never forget how you felt as a child, but you can control your responses to those events now as an adult. That is one of the objectives of doing exercises. Another is to remember the abuse so that you're no longer frightened of it and will be able to discover ways of confronting your abuser about it. You have all the facts now, so to speak.

The Affective Memory Exercise is called "affective" (not "effective") because it deals with the feelings or *affects* that come up from reliving an important past experience. Actors are always looking for the truth of a moment, so they often take real, emotionally laden or life-altering events from their own lives and use that material to recreate similar emotional situations for their characters.

Famous acting coach Stella Adler once told a class that in order to truly experience the full awareness of a particular moment, Marlon Brando once picked up a ringing telephone at her house, listened into the receiver, heard the person on the other end, and then said nothing as the other person must have spouted on and on. Brando then, just as abruptly, hung up the receiver without saying a word. When Stella asked him why he had not carried on a two-way conversation with the caller, Brando answered simply, "I just wanted to know what complete boredom felt like." In other words, Brando wanted to be able to recreate the inner experience of boredom in a character some day. Knowing actors as I do, he probably put that feeling away somewhere inside for the time when he would use it in a part. The truth of a moment on the stage is felt by an audience only if the actor is able to really feel those emotions himself.

Actors use the Affective Memory Exercise only in a scene that requires immediate dramatic reactions, an instance when they have no build-up time to create these emotions. For instance, if another character suddenly comes onto the stage and announces, "My Lord, the King is dead!" the actor may need to experience shock and disbelief as the character or may be required to burst into tears upon hearing the news. But the actor playing this scene might really be feeling pretty good, couldn't care less about a "king," and may not be able to find these negative emotions right then and there. However, in order for the actor as the character to look genuinely affected by the news, the actor must find something upsetting in his or her own real life in order to connect with the emotional state needed to play that scene believably.

So, the Affective Memory Exercise is very useful in helping you involve all your senses working together to recreate a very dramatic event in your life. Remember this exercise is the most emotionally involving of all, so speak only about feelings and stay on track by focusing on tactile images rather than talking in full sentences, unless of course you have opted to simply tell the story and describe the emotions rather than actually feel them.

The Affective Memory Exercise

1. Find a comfortable chair and sit in it, relaxing and emptying your mind.

2. Keep your "third eye" open by reminding yourself you are giving yourself permission to do this exercise, but that you can stop it at any time and go back to the Relaxation (Sunshine) Exercise, or simply stop it altogether and go back to other exercises before you attempt this one again.
3. Now, begin to allow yourself to remember the abuse situation moment by moment as it happened. Keep focused on sensory feelings by continuously asking yourself the questions you are now familiar with, including "What is right in front of me?" You may say, "I see blue, a kind of green-blue, and I smell mist in the air," or "I feel cold all over."
4. Begin now to see in your mind's eye the place where the abuse occurred. Just look around the room or the space where it happened.
5. Continue telling your story sensorially. What do you see? Answer sensorially. You might say, "I see bright lights." Or "I see purple. It seems to be glowing." Or "Everything looks dull, lifeless, dark."
6. Speak out loud about what kind of air or atmosphere you sense here. You might say something like, "It smells fetid, stale." Or "It smells like cooking, pungent and strong cooking odors."
7. Continue to the next sense, perhaps your sense of hearing. What do you hear? Voices? Doors opening or closing? The sound of someone walking or running?
8. At this time you might see a person or someone in the room or space with you. Your friend or acting coach might ask, "Who is it?" Then you can answer, "Dad," "Mom," or whomever you see. Continue to describe your experience sensorially. How does the person look. How are they acting? You might say, "He (or she) looks sad, crying. I can't really see their face."
9. Now ask yourself what he (or she) is doing? Sensorially respond: "I see a glass. Now I smell liquor, and it's getting closer to me." Or "I hear soft words." Describe how you feel. "I feel sick to my stomach," or "My head aches." Stop. Check yourself. Can you continue? Or is the exercise becoming overwhelming?
10. If you can continue, watch what is happening in your mind's eye. What about your sense of taste? Is your mouth dry from fear?
11. Pretend the past is now. Keep going through the abuse situation as it unfolds as best you can. You have probably told this story to therapists and friends, but now you are telling it to yourself. Keep focused on sensory feelings by using adjectives and feeling words such as "cold, sweaty," etc., rather than nouns such as "chair" or "wall" so you can get back to that place and discover your emotions.

Remember that by involving ourselves thoroughly in sensory tasks, the form and feeling of the place takes care of itself. And by using our senses in this very focused, very definite time and place, we can remember what happened in the abuse situation and the aftereffects it caused. Continue with what you see, hear, smell, or touch.

12. Describe now the sense of touch you have. Begin to feel whatever material is around you from the past as if it were in the present. You might say, "I feel material on my hand, like wool. It's soft and fur-like." Or you might say, "I feel skin next to my face and it feels slimy." Ask yourself, "What is the texture of the rug, the cloth of the bedding, or the feel of the curtains." Remember always to keep your touch about an inch above any real material so that you are working in your imagination, but sensorially recreating the feelings. Speak the sense memories out loud.

    Again, you don't have to get overly graphic in your mind's eye. But you probably can remember what happened and begin to deal with it now, as an older person. The feeling you had as a child can now be comforted by you the adult.

13. Describe sensorially as much as you can. Remember about where the abuse occurred, and remember to answer not by saying "I see the bed," but instead saying, "I see yellow and white" (which may have been the bedpost and the pillows). How did the abuse occur? Do you remember the circumstances surrounding it? Just keep asking yourself out loud, "What can I hear? See? Taste? Smell? Feel?" Keep focused on who was there, who was not there, who might have heard the commotion of your abuse, who couldn't have heard it.

14. What about your neighbors? Did they suspect? Why didn't they do anything about it?

15. Now **stop.** Go to your pad of paper or your tape recorder and describe all the feelings—disgust, worry, anger, fear, or sadness—that you can. Could you ever go back to the place where you were abused? How do you think you would act or react now, after doing this exercise? Do you feel you could confront the abuser now? Why?

Remember, the more you do an Affective Memory exercise, the more you will remember specific events, objects, people, or facts about the abuse. For survivors, the immediacy of the abuse might seem to be looming just under the surface many times during your everyday life. At any given moment a gesture, conversation, or experience can trigger the memories of the abuser, the abuse, and your powerlessness and helplessness. The Affective Memory Exercise will help you capture this immediacy and put it in the past. The exercise will finally allow you to see the whole picture of the abuse event. You will be able to deal with the acute emotions emanating from your memories, neutralize them, and integrate them in such a way that they can no longer plague you or stop you from your success and accomplishment in your present life.

Henry's Story

Henry was a twenty-one-year-old actor when he first came to see me complaining of not being able to get over leg pain after he fell on a set while trying to do his own stunts during a shoot of his popular series. Henry had craggy good looks that always landed him parts in crime stories. But when I asked him where the scars actually came from, Henry could not remember. He never believed he had been physically abused. The scars and cuts he clearly saw on his skin must have had some other explanation, he said.

Henry's psychiatrist had used talk therapy to help him look at his past. That therapy brought up many memories of his father's explosive temper. But after years of this kind of therapy, all the while rationalizing his father's cruelty and his mother's denial that anything untoward was happening in her family, Henry was ready to find out what really happened. Why, for instance, had the X-rays taken after his fall showed old broken bones in many places? His limbs looked as if he had been in a war. In fact, Henry could not remember his childhood at all. All he could remember, he said, was school, where teachers noticed he was belligerent, fighting at the drop of a hat with other boys. He also remembered his father "busting up the house" many times when he came home. But outside of those few, spotty memories, a large part of Henry's past remained a mystery.

When Henry came to therapy with me, we began doing acting exercises. These were made easier due to the fact that Henry was an actor. He appeared to be delighted to get acting training at the acting institute and acting exercises in his therapy. He was able to work on them at home alone, too. He was set. As he became more and more adept at recreating and experiencing his feelings, he landed a small role in a movie. He was to play a gangster who dies in the middle of a heist. The film was actually a comedy, and Henry certainly had not planned on getting serious.

But during one of the rehearsals, his character was shot, and Henry fell on the floor. As he lay "dying," he suddenly and abruptly "smelled the rotten stench of hotdogs . . . like hotdogs that have been out in the sun for too long." This memory and its incumbent feelings brought back a vivid scene of his father slapping him and punching him while Henry was on the floor. The father had been "boozing and eating dogs" while watching a football game on television. Henry remembers he was "about six years old," had been playing with a ball in the house, and had accidentally bumped his father's chair. That chain of events released tremendous anger from his father, who then proceeded to beat Henry unconscious. Henry was concerned because he remembered this flashback scene of his past right on the set, in front of the camera! The reexperience in acting frightened Henry, and we began the Affective Memory Exercise.

As Henry sat on my couch, he first began using his sense of smell, which can be one of the most powerfully evocative senses that humans have, and was the one that originally triggered his recall. He began remembering the smell of cookies, junk food, and the odor of rotten food in his house. His home was always "filthy," and he remembered that on one particular day his father had lost his job or some money and had come home early in a "crappy mood."

The father had slapped his wife, Henry's mother, and she had fled the kitchen and locked herself in the bedroom. Henry remembers hearing crying, sobbing, doors slamming, and the sight of the red of his father's face and then the red of blood. He remembered being terrified and asking his father for a cookie, thinking that a simple question would take the father out of his furor and bring him back to a simple reality. But that didn't work. His father became more enraged and turned on Henry. Henry remembered pain in his arm, excruciating pain. Then he recalled memories of white . . . white walls, white uniforms, white doors. As he described his experience, he began to remember the odors and smells of chloroform or alcohol, he was too young to know the difference. Then he remembered the feel of starched white sheets. It's the first time he said he ever remembers feeling too clean. Then isolated pictures came into his mind of a sweet face with red lips, soft sounds of a voice, and a kind pat on his cheek.

Henry stopped the exercise at this time. He opened his eyes and looked at me as if incredulous. He now remembered that someone next door had called an ambulance and people had taken him to the hospital. There, nurses and doctors had kindly patched him up and had given him toys and even ice cream. He remembered that while being given pain medication, he was allowed to watch television and get goodies from "ladies who came around with carts and carts of toys. I thought it was Christmas time." He was not returned home—instead he was sent to live with foster parents who had two other children. He never saw his real mother again.

As he told me the story he began crying. He said later that he had never cried like that in his life . . . long, sorrowful sobs. But to him, the emotion did not come from remembering his abuse, but from the fact that he had wanted to go home those many years ago! Abused children often would rather stay with an abusive real parent than leave and live with kind strangers.

In the next few months, Henry discovered his mother had died. But no one could tell him how. He found his father, now an old man in a county treatment center. His father, now well into his eighties, could not remember Henry. He tried to remind his father of who he was, bring back some of the past, but the old man simply told Henry he loved him.

As he left the home, Henry found a sense of freedom. He knew the truth, he had experienced the feelings as an adult, and he could finally know what happened to him and go forward in his life. His movie came out; he was successful as an actor, and he reports his life has changed considerably now that he is married with a child of his own. He fears he is overprotecting his son, but he is overcoming that worry by discovering lessons of good parenting in a class he and his wife attend weekly.

The Preparation-Before-a-Scene exercise in the chapter that follows is the very last exercise we do, and it entails a kind of "rehearsal" for when you will confront your abuser. It's the same kind of rehearsal an actor uses to prepare him or herself to go on stage or in front of a camera to do a scene.

Chapter 24

Preparation-Before-a-Scene

The Final Stretch

Well, here we are at the last exercise, the Preparation-Before-a-Scene Exercise. You might be wondering, "What are we preparing for?" As you may have already guessed, we are and have been preparing you for a confrontation with your abuser—either personally or in your mind. Or, if the abuser is deceased, at his or her grave. If there is no grave, then wherever the person died is the place where you might consider your confrontation. The site of confrontation is very important because where the person died probably happened in your adulthood, and the actual abuse took place in your childhood. Remember, you are confronting that person now, as an adult.

Just try not to make your confrontation where the abuse occurred. There are good reasons for this. For one, the place where you were abused will take you back in your mind to a childlike place, somewhere where you once again might feel powerlessness and vulnerable. That's not what we want. The power and control you have practiced in these exercises have been accomplished so that you can feel like an adult when you confront your abuser. Confronting the abuser wherever he or she is now in your adulthood will aid you in taking command of who you are and what you want now.

The Preparation-Before-a-Scene Exercise is a warm-up exercise in the same way that marathon runners train to get used to the track and build stamina for their final run. This exercise will help you get ready for your marathon: to confront your abuser, but this time as an adult who will be able to acknowledge your feelings and deal with the trauma in an adaptive rather than sabotaging way.

In the Affective Memory Exercise, your focus was inward, discovering all the intricacies of what happened during your abuse. Now your focus will be outward, so you will need to answer important questions that will catapult you forward in your quest for inner peace and closure.

Ask yourself at this point, "How do I feel about confronting my abuser?" Just ask the question and wait for a moment to see what feelings come up. Then ask, "Am I skeptical that this will work out the way I hope or anticipate?" "Am I frightened still of the abuser or what my own anger will generate if I ever do see that person again?" "Am I eager to get this over with, to really let them have it and tell them how I feel?" Or are you spiritual about seeing and confronting the abuser? You might say to yourself, "It will be worth it or it won't; it's out of my hands."

When actors prepare to go on the stage or in front of a camera to do a particular scene, they always have to ask themselves a series of questions that are answered mentally. These questions are:

1. Who am I?
2. What do I want?
3. What is in the way of me getting what I want?
4. How do I overcome the obstacle standing in my way, so that I can get what I want?

In order to answer these four tough questions, an actor usually uses many of the exercises you just did. They then continue to ask themselves even *more* questions, such as:

- What are the circumstances surrounding this scene? In other words, what is going on in this scene right now—what am I coming in on?
- What are the immediate surroundings? Are you going to the abuser's home, etc.?
- What is my relationship with the other characters? In your situation, you might ask, " What was/is my relationship with the abuser?"

For abuse survivors these questions are very important. Now, as you focus outward, you will need to answer these questions in a linear way based on what you know about yourself, the abuser, and your relationship with him or her. As you ask each of the four questions, you will find that many other questions come to mind. Try not to go to the next question before you have fully answered the one you have just asked yourself.

The Preparation-Before-a-Scene Exercise

1. Sit in a chair and be sure you are relaxed. Keep your eyes closed and speak your answers out loud.

2. Ask yourself, "Who am I?" But unlike an actor playing a role, this question asks you to look inside at who you are now as an adult. So answer in ways that will direct you to look at **you** and how you are today. How old are you now? Where do you live at this present time? What city? What part of town? What do you do for work? Are you a student? Where? What are you studying? Whom do you live with at this time—alone or with a roommate or pet? Do you have a romantic relationship? Are you married? Do you have children? Who are your friends? Enemies? Work associates? What activities do you participate in now? Are you sedate—like a writer—or active—a sports person? Are you religious? Do you go to a church, synagogue, or mosque regularly? Where do you find your friends? Or are you a loner? How do you picture yourself—kind, happy, worried all the time, sad, jumpy, unpredictable, impulsive, slow? How do you think others picture you?

3. Now ask yourself, "What do I want?" Be specific. Do you want to address or confront the abuser? Why? How do you feel that will help? If you don't want to confront him or her, why not? Make your answer specific to dealing with your abuser on some level. Equally important is how you plan to confront: Face-to-face? On the phone? Writing a letter? Do you plan to knock on his or her door one day unexpectedly? List all possible scenarios in a linear way here also, again based on what you already know about the abuser and his or her habits. By making this list complete, you will again be taking control of how you can manage this meeting—what is possible, what is not possible.

4. Now ask yourself, "What are the circumstances of my life right now and my abuser's life?" In other words, do you and the abuser live in the same place, same city, same part of town? Is the abuser alive or dead? If alive, do you have any connection with him or her at all, even through other family members? What is that connection? Adversarial? Do you connect with him or her to fight with them or to make them feel guilty? Do you make sure at family gatherings that you are never near the abuser? Is the abuser married now, possibly with children of his or her own? Is there a real chance the abuser is abusing his or her own kids? Or is the abuser old and infirm or suffering with illness such as Alzheimer's or a stroke? Will he or she even remember you and what happened? All circumstances surrounding your ability to confront your abuser are important in this question.

5. Ask, "What is in my way of confronting my abuser?" Are you afraid the abuser will deny his or her abuse of you? What would you do if that were to happen? This is a very important question because it forces you to look at how you will be able to accomplish your goal of confrontation. What might be in your way could be something as simple as the abuser not admitting that anything wrong happened and refusing to listen to you. Or worse, insisting that everything you accuse him or her of is a

figment of your imagination; or that you were so young you don't remember accurately. This is a common scenario for abuse survivors. The abuser might have dementia and have forgotten who you are. Perhaps the abuser was in a position of authority, a teacher or religious leader, who had access to many children, and you were just one of them. Travel and distance might be a factor in your getting to the place where you will be able to confront. In fact, any obstacle in your way should be spoken about out loud.

6. Ask yourself, "What do I do to overcome this obstacle?" Really brainstorm out loud. Where do you plan to have this meeting take place? If it is travel and distance that will impede your getting there, how can you get to where the abuser is? Is it financially feasible? If you still feel tremendous fear or trepidation in confronting, how will you overcome that obstacle? Would it help if someone else came with you to the meeting with your abuser? Who? Does that person believe you? As you probably already know, so much denial exists in families where abuse occurred that often other family members, even those who were also abused, simply want to forget about it, pretend it's over and say they are getting on with their lives. Comments like those can add to your anxiety.

7. Finally, close your eyes and picture your abuser then and now (if you know what he or she looks like now). Picture confronting him or her. Go through how it will happen moment by moment. Take control and notice at what point you feel anxiety. At what point do you feel strong in your story of how this confrontation will come about? Be specific. What do you fantasize will happen? Will your confrontation be successful? What do you expect, and what do you imagine is possible? Will the person be sorry and contrite, argumentative, still a bully? What if the abuser denies it? How do you imagine you will feel?

8. Do as much as you can, then stop. Go to your pad and write down your feelings or record on your tape recorder all emotions or thoughts about how you feel you can (or perhaps right now, cannot) confront your abuser.

Just as an actor, you have now come to your big moment. And you're prepared for it. But after all these years and doing all these exercises, what do you really think will happen? Suppose you decide you are not up for the task? Will you give yourself permission not to find and confront the abuser? That is certainly one option. If you choose not to, how will you deal with how you feel about the abuser?

Once you work through the beginnings of your rehearsal for your confrontation with the Preparation-Before-a-Scene Exercise, you will notice an increase in your level of understanding of the pathology in your family that made the abuse come about in the first place. You will also have an ability to learn the historical facts that you needed then in order to take care of yourself now. You will probably realize, for instance, that daddy saying "All daddies do this to their daughters" is wrong. But you will not just understand this on an intellectual level (where, of course, you know it), but also on an *emotional* level as well, where you might still be trying to justify your father's actions. Your old, familiar patterns will be discarded for new, more positive ones.

For actors, doing these preparations before a scene means that they now know why their character is going into the scene, what they need to accomplish in that scene, and why they will be leaving the scene after they have accomplished the objective.

So, just as actors ask themselves, "What happened to my character before the scene?" you, too, will be examining all the factors of your life, the players and situations in it that led up to the abuse and trauma.

Remember, the Preparation-Before-a-Scene Exercise includes recalling the entire history of your relationship with the people in your life, including the abuser, siblings, other family members, school friends, etc. But it also includes remembering the environment of the scene—the time of day, the physical objects in the scene, who the character (you) is about to meet with, and what you (the character) hopes to accomplish in this scene.

It doesn't matter what the abuser admits or doesn't admit. All that really matters is that *you* know what happened and that you took control over how you confronted, or decided not to confront, your abuser.

You have now become an actor in your own life . . . the play of your life. Preparing has been a particularly important aspect of overcoming the aftereffects of your abuse. Prepare well so that the experience itself will flow smoothly and under control.

Part Four

Putting It All Together and Living Your Life

Chapter 25

How Abuse Affects Relationships: The 20 Most Common Relationship Problems

Do Different Abuses Affect Adult Relationships Differently?

I am often asked if sexual, physical, or emotional abuse in childhood contributes to a particular kind of abuse in adult relationships. Do survivors who have been hit, beaten, or physically threatened in childhood by an older child or an aggressive, out-of-control, or substance-abusing adult unconsciously seek a similar relationship in a lover? Does an adult who has been abused as a child seek a relationship where their partner has all the power? Many therapists agree that the answers are "yes" to these questions much of the time, although the extent of the damage depends upon so many things. For example, was the abuse pre-verbal (before the child could put the experience into words), or post-verbal? Different child abuse experiences will dictate different behavior patterns in adult relationships.

Ask yourself some questions about your adult relationships: Are your relationships marred with mistrust and fear, and do you rely on escape tactics in order to feel confident? What are escape tactics? Are they ways you devise to make sure that you can always get out of a relationship unscathed, without too much pain? Some escape tactics are: finding fault with a person or lover so that if they break up with you, you won't feel so bad, or trying to find things about them that you don't like so that you don't feel so pulled into them, and won't feel helpless if they ever leave you. Perhaps your parent or caregiver withheld important information from you when you were a child, leaving you with the feeling that you've been missing out on something all your life. Many adoptees who were never told they were adopted may experience this type of mistrust, a nagging feeling that something is missing. It's so important that adult caregivers are honest with children.

Some of the most frequently asked questions in therapy are: "Am I doing something I don't know about that makes abusers come to me?" Or, "Why do I feel so guilty all the time, as though I'm the bad person in this relationship? Why do I feel like I'm the one to blame for relationships going sour?" Adults abused as children are often so ready to take the blame for their failed relationships that they don't realize that they are blaming the victim—themselves. But if you are the victim of abuse, *you are not to blame*. And, if you have never experienced anything but abuse, how can you look for and find a loving, kind relationship? How would you even know what to look for?

Not all people experience abuse in the same way. Not all sexual abuse survivors have terrible aftereffects, and some survivors who appear to be *least* abused can suffer the most serious problems in later relationships. Other survivors seem unfazed and can have good sexual relationships with their partners

If you were emotionally abused in childhood, the abuse may have been much more subtle than either sexual or physical abuse. Emotional abuse may occur when a child or adolescent is not heard or respected or when their needs and wants are neglected—they are left dirty or hungry, or left alone much of the time to be abused by strangers, or left in some other kind of danger. Emotionally abused children often grow up believing that they are no good, that there is something lacking in them that caused others to disrespect them and not care for them. The child is confused: "Did I do something to make my parents hate me?"

In the case of Harold, his mother repeatedly told him that she hated him because an older sister had died before Harold's birth. The mother had wanted that child instead of Harold. How could he know this or understand why he was being held responsible for his mother's irrational hatred? The child constantly experienced his mother's disappointment.

Some survivors have a strong denial system so that the aftereffects of their abuse visit them in ways other than in relationship problems. They may have problems at work or in their inability to feel light and carefree. After attempting some of the exercises in this book, you may have noticed that certain aftereffects of abuse have become blatantly clear and show up in your behavior toward others.

What's Missing in Your Relationship?

How can you sympathize or care about anyone when all you can think about is yourself and your pain? How can you empathize with others when no one has ever had any empathy for you? What stands in the way of your attaining a rich, loving relationship? Do you build up expectations with potential lovers? How can you protect yourself from being hurt by rejection or surprised that your anticipation of what the relationship will be like is completely off track? How can you react moment to moment and discover the good and bad of the relationship as it unfolds?

Are you jealous, mistrustful, scared, withholding, unable to share feelings and affection, avoidant (avoiding difficult aspects of the relationships, such as conflicts), shy, or unsure in a love relationship? One result of learning more about how you connect with others through using acting techniques is that you can, once and for all, truly relax and describe yourself to others. Breaking the secrecy of your abuse means you are actually *doing* something about the abuse—you have begun to speak the truth out loud and that is the beginning of true relationships with other people.

Complications usually occur when you take on the whole responsibility for what's wrong in your relationship. Isn't the relationship supposed to be fifty-fifty? What is often missing is give-and-take, good communication between partners, an understanding of the other person's point of view, and the ability to realize that another person's personality is different from yours. The way they think is different from the way you think.

Any relationship comes with two people bringing their baggage from their families of origin into it. If one or both partners were abused in childhood, they often blame themselves when the relationship goes wrong. They do not see the give-and-take needed to have a successful relationship because they may feel the abuse caused them to be intrinsically bad. The responsibility for success in any relationship cannot rely on only one partner. Both need to be empathic and recognize how each person's behavior affects the other. That's one way survivors can empower themselves—by realizing that they are an equal partner and not be dumped on.

How Is Abuse Affecting Your Relationship

Before going on to the relationship (communication) exercises that can begin to repair the damage done by early abuse experiences, let's look at the nineteen most common relationship problems and where they come from

The Nineteen Most Common Relationship Problems

1. Mistrust of intimacy, hypervigilance, and jealousy
2. Numbing out and dissociating
3. Not wanting to be touched
4. Somaticizing

5. Feeling trapped and trying to escape
6. Sexual dysfunctions and fetishes
7. Friendship to escape from intimacy
8. Using the relationship to acquire an identity
9. Fantasizing a lover in order to remain isolated and unhurt
10. Creating your own personality with fantasy
11. Sexualizing relationships where no sex exists
12. Crushes and other power reducers
13. Lying and the desire to be seen differently
14. Talking against your lover
15. Manipulating the relationship with money or power
16. Sleeping with many partners when in a monogamous relationship
17. Prematurely leaving the relationship (or, splitting revisited)
18. Alcohol, drugs, and other addictions
19. Bullying
20. Recreating the abuse situation

Hypervigilance, Jealousy, and Mistrust of Intimacy

Your lack of ability to trust yourself in your love choices may be the first indication that some type of abuse probably occurred in your childhood. That lack of trust may prevent you from involving yourself in an intimate, lasting relationship. Often, when a relationship appears to be getting too close, too intimate and too "perfect," abuse survivors actively look for and find ways of mistrusting their partners so that they won't be devastated if the person were to leave them.

How can you trust another person when you're not sure what you are looking for? How can you trust yourself that what you see is really there? Most abuse survivors in my practice complain that they are just waiting for their relationships, love or otherwise, to fall apart—as if they have no control over the outcome at all.

Where It Comes From

As you might have already guessed, mistrust comes from the earliest betrayal by the abuser. As a child, you undoubtedly trusted the main adults in your life. You thought all adults must be trustworthy simply because they were bigger and smarter than you. At that time you were not able to control the assault on your body and/or soul, and you depended on trusting a caretaker for your very existence. When the adult confused you by abusing that trust, you were left not knowing why. The promise you made yourself after your abuse—of always being careful not to trust others—has probably prevented you from trusting an adult relationship.

Real trust begins as you discover you can exist and care for yourself without someone else dictating to you how to live your life. Overcoming powerlessness is so . . . empowering.

When your trust of your parent was first violated, you may have suffered hypervigilance, a form of fear where you are constantly panicked that something out of your control will occur. This hypervigilance can translate into a startle response—always jumping up and never finding calm and peacefulness in anything, much less a relationship.

It takes conscious effort for survivors to begin to trust that they can live their own lives effectively. Before they can trust others, they must trust themselves.

Jealousy and lack of self-worth come from messages others gave us that we were not good enough or couldn't measure up to someone else. The anger, inspired by trying to live up to others' expectations, spawns competitiveness in adulthood. The abuse you suffered can make you feel that if you had been "better" or "different" the abusiveness would not have occurred. That feeling of it being our own fault is a way to take control over the abuser, but it also makes us jealous of nonabused people. We may think, "Why me?" or "Why were they better?"

Numbing Out and Dissociating

Numbing out during sex may be an unconscious cry for autonomy or control over your own body. Remember, you probably told yourself you would never again allow anyone to force you to feel sexual without your permission. At least when you feel nothing, when all emotions and sexual feelings become numb, you have that control. Especially, this may be an attempt not to experience your lover as your abuser.

Problems arise when you want others to be a part of your pleasure. Fear and the desire to control your sexuality can prevent letting your lover become part of your life. Instead, you may try to blame your partner for unsatisfying sex encounters. If only your partner were less selfish in bed or a better lover, you think you would find pleasure. It's important for you to investigate numbing out.

Where It Comes From

Numbing out and dissociating are used unconsciously as important protective devises against intimacy. When you were abused, you may have put your mind somewhere else in order not to feel the humiliation and fear that threatened to overwhelm you. Now that you don't need this defense against intimacy anymore, it's important to notice how and when it happens and begin to find new ways to connect to a lover.

Not Wanting to Be Touched

Unwanted touch heightens feelings of helplessness, making you feel that your body doesn't belong to you. And that can be a reason for dissociation in a relationship. If you can't physically control your body, you will try to emotionally take charge of it by separating from it.

Survivors who have been inappropriately touched may describe many more and much stronger unwanted aftereffects than those who have been beaten, penetrated sexually, or emotionally destroyed by verbal attacks. They don't know why being touched brings up so much shyness and disgust. Embarrassment and disgust at feeling *they* have the sick mind adds to the survivor's confusion about why a touch would feel bad. But these emotions are the result of feeling powerlessness over whoever touched you as a child. So when you want a relationship where touch is welcomed, the old feelings and memories of disgust might interfere with a healthy, open, touching partnership.

Where It Comes From

Unwanted touching was what probably happened during your abuse experiences. When we have no control over who is attacking our bodies, we want to make sure that when we are adults no one can touch it without our express permission. A psychology student I knew, herself a physical abuse survivor, was sensitive to this and always made sure she asked people first, "May I touch you?" before she would hug them or connect with them physically.

Somatization

The psychological phenomenon called "somatization" fits right into this modality. Somatization is when people translate their emotional pain into physical pain. Many survivors cannot face the fact of who abused them, the circumstances of the abuse, or their resulting fear and anger. They're afraid they will never get over it, so instead of dealing with the psychological trauma, they focus on their physical symptoms.

Wher it Comes From

Although many of these pains are real and have a true physical reason for existing, they also offer an excuse for not making love. In fact, saying no may feel like the only real control a survivor retains: "No, I can't make love—it hurts too much" instead of "No, I'll make love when I want to and the way I want to."

Of course, some people have real physical abnormalities or problems that need medical attention. (If you do suffer pain during intercourse or sexual contact, be sure to contact your doctor. And make sure you are sedated before any painful or uncomfortable procedures are done to remedy your problem. That will prevent a traumatic reexperiencing of your abuse from occurring.) But keep in mind: it's often easier for abuse survivors to simply find a *physical* reason for not connecting physically to another person than it is to deal with the real reason behind their somatizations.

Feeling pains in your body during sex may be a metaphor for trying to be heard by others about your abuse, a call for the help you were not able to get as a child. Freud felt that we remain at the stage of development we were at when a trauma took place. If that is true, then abuse survivors probably act the way they did then, and the pain they felt during their abuse is now being expressed through their bodies instead of through words. That's why it's so important to connect mind with body.

Feeling Trapped and Trying to Escape

Physicality, sex, or trust can trigger another fear for adult abuse survivors: fear of being trapped in what appears to them to be a frightening situation. Researchers have referred to this phenomenon as "learned helplessness," the feeling that no matter what you do to escape, you won't be able to.

I've known actors who'd get on the stage in front of an audience and suddenly become dizzy or experience a full-blown panic attack because they felt that once they were out there, they literally couldn't escape. How could they break character and announce to an audience, "Sorry, folks, I can't stay out here, I'm feeling sick"? They felt trapped, just as survivors felt trapped by their abusers.

Often survivors and performers described similar fears in relationships: meeting someone they are attracted to but then panicking that the person will get too close and that they won't be able to get away. Feeling trapped can increase the fear that you are at your partner's beck and call—the last place survivors want to be.

Where It Comes From

On some primitive level I think most survivors realize that feeling trapped, stuck, or unable to escape is the exact feeling they experienced during their abuse. The bigger, more powerful abuser was able to say or do whatever he or she wanted to, and the survivor was a captive. No amount of struggling or trying to escape helped free them from their terror. They were forced to feel unwanted, often unexpected orgasms, and the incumbent shame, humiliation, and disgrace that came with this helplessness. So, when you do get serious about a partner, these old feelings push their way into your consciousness and prevent you from staying and communicating honestly.

Sexual Dysfunctions and Fetishes

Trouble enjoying sexual relationships is a hallmark of sexual, physical, and emotional abuse. Some dysfunctions can be exclusively psychological in nature with survivors having constant concerns about the ability to have an orgasm or needing to take substances to get sexually excited. Other problems include physical symptoms or the need to think of *fetishes*, which are objects or nongenital parts of the body that cause an habitual erotic or sexual response or fixation, in order to become sexually aroused.

Where It Comes From

Fetishes are usually accidentally learned at the time the abuse takes place. I say "accidentally" because I am describing what psychologists call "classical conditioning." This phenomenon occurs when one behavior is paired with another that may or may not be related to the first. But because the two behaviors occurred at approximately the same time, they become inextricably connected to each other in the mind forever—like Pavlov's dog. The dog would salivate when he heard a bell because initially the bell was rung at the same time red meat was presented to him. The two things became tightly linked in the dog's mind.

The same phenomenon occurs in fetishes. If your attention was drawn to a particular part of the abuser's body at the time of your abuse, then later on that part of someone's body might trigger sexual arousal. You know that something is wrong, doesn't feel right, or just feels "bad."

When a child is made to feel sexual, or when physical punishment becomes sexual, a child may split off whatever he or she sees—hand, a boot, muscles (what psychoanalysts call "a part object") and that object or body part will forever represent the first sexual excitement the child encountered. Later in life, when the survivor wants to see a "whole" person as a sexual object, they might find that it is only the fetish (the muscle or boots) that turns them on sexually, not their lover. This can be very disconcerting. The powerlessness of not being turned on by what you want to find exciting is humiliating and often embarrassing.

But these dysfunctions, although they will always be the first line of fire of excitement, do not need to be the only line of excitement. You can find other things that excite you and begin to train yourself to be excited by those new discoveries. For example, in their book *Courage to Heal*, authors Ellen Bass and Laura Davis suggest you begin to turn your sexual fetish or dysfunction around by no longer masturbating while thinking about the sexual or physical abuse.

Friendship to Escape from Intimacy

A friendship feels safe and has definite boundaries that are comfortable. Even if the friendship proves unstable, you may think, "Who cares—get more friends." Being friends can feel easy; you can be "yourself" when the sexual component is removed.

Some abuse survivors are very afraid of being enveloped or swallowed up in a love relationship. Or they fear the responsibility of having to be faithful and always there for another person. They feel overwhelmed by commitment. My friend Jeffrey used to brag, "I make a great friend; I'm no good in relationships."

But you, a survivor, probably do want a long-term, loving relationship. The problem may be that you feel so insecure about love that you will choose to make a friend of the person you would like as a lover, or make a lover out of someone who really is only your friend. Topsy-turvy, but safe. When you have no self-esteem, no sense of your worth, a friend will be someone you can talk to, confide in. You don't have to worry about how you will be perceived by a friend, the way you would as a lover.

Because a lover may appear to be more like the abuser, a love relationship is more threatening than a friendship, even though settling for a friendship instead of what you really want might make you feel like you've "chickened out" or let yourself down. A love relationship might feel shaming to you because shame is what "love" felt like in childhood.

Other abuse survivors settle for any partner they can find, and love has nothing to do with it. They believe they are lucky to have any relationship at all. They feel their child abuse has permanently damaged them physically and psychologically, so they don't think they deserve a good relationship. My client A.C. reported to me that her brother, an angry, unhappy man who emotionally taunted her in their childhood, told her, "You're going to have to take whatever guy comes along. You aren't cute enough to pick and choose." All too often, survivors feel that because they are damaged, they won't be able to find anyone to truly love them—so friendship is the next best thing. They feel that if a less desirable partner is all that is available to them, they better grab him or her now. That is how so many survivors end up with batterers, substance abusers, two-timers, and other undesirables.

Some survivors use being "too nice" in a relationship (see chapter 2). But being too nice is also a distancing tactic to avoid intimacy, a way of keeping someone at arm's length and not letting them get too near because you still fear closeness. But being too nice is mostly a way of hiding the shame you feel.

Where It Comes From

One unique way survivors find safety and retain self-respect in relationships is to create a sexual relationship with someone who they really will always see only as a friend. That way, they can retain and control their sexual feelings, never giving themselves up to someone who could hurt them the way the abuser did. If you don't have romantic feelings and sexual fantasies for your lover, you shouldn't be surprised when he or she ends the romantic relationship.

Some abuse survivors pursue dull, uninteresting lovers and then complain about how they can't find interesting relationships. That opens the door for them to feel secure and not in jeopardy of losing someone they truly love.

Maybe you're afraid you will not be able to maintain a wild, passionate love affair without it soon turning stagnant. All relationships are boring at some point and they get exciting at other times. But abuse survivors have no template for how relationships naturally ebb and flow. They only imagine how it is *supposed* to happen, and they worry how it will end.

Low self-esteem and low self-image is another impediment to forming a loving, trusting relationship. Turning potential lovers into friends before things get too complicated is an effective escape from the fear of not deserving to have a love partner. And friendships certainly can prevent that frightening feeling of being rejected sexually.

If you are an abuse survivor, you may feel you are surrounding yourself with a veil of protection by denying yourself the love you really want, but what you are probably getting is a feeling of loneliness and isolation. The exercises will help you trust yourself to take a chance.

Using the Relationship to Acquire an Identity

Do you wonder, "Who am I?" "What do I want?" "What will make me happy, secure, trusting, and successful?" Sometimes survivors get into relationships they know are not permanent in order to experiment with feelings like these to see what will transpire. When we have no idea what a relationship is, what it means, and what might be expected from it, we often "try on" many relationships to see if one "fits" our personality. Like going shopping for clothes, we try to discover the kind of relationship we want without knowing first what we need from it. A lot of time and energy can be spent looking when all the time, in our unconscious mind, we know what we need but don't feel ready to get it.

Some relationships are transitional—you take them while you are waiting to feel ready to commit fully to someone else. If both of you feel the same way, no one will get hurt. It's only when you try to change or mold this person into someone else that problems arise. The Inner Monologue Exercise will help you reflect on what you want by helping you actively hear yourself.

Where It Comes From

One of the most anger-provoking remarks that can be made to anyone is "you are nothing." But abuse survivors are especially vulnerable to the indignity of that remark because all their lives they've felt so suggestible. Their very identities can be formed and changed by the whims and casual remarks of other people. People are always ready to critique you if you are willing to stand around and drink it in. Originally, your abuser most likely made you feel beneath contempt, as if you were a "nothing," a person to be used and then thrown away. Your deep fear that the abuser was right takes over. When we don't know who we are, how others view us has a huge impact. The identity exercises can help—the Private Moment Exercise, the Building-a-Room Exercise, and the Portrait Exercise—will all help you look inward at your own process and how you perceive the world. You may be surprised to see how strong your own opinions, needs, and wants are.

Fantasizing a Lover in Order to Remain Isolated and Unhurt

Anything that isn't real is a fantasy. Fantasy comes in many forms and shapes, and there are many facets to fantasy. Anxiety is usually fear about what *will* happen in the future—and that is a fantasy. Your worst fears are usually never realized, are they? Fantasy works a lot of magic in relationships. For one thing, if you are into fantasy, a relationship can appear to come out perfectly. But if it doesn't, you can simply change your fantasy so that it will. It's always easier to fantasize relationships than to experience them. That way, you have control over them. But when you try to mold a real person to fit into your fantasy relationship, you will undoubtedly become frustrated when the other person's real personality emerges.

Everyone has fantasized a sexual encounter that was tailor-made to their specifications—what the partner would say or do in bed, where the sex would take place—and most people would agree that these are fun (and normal) thought processes. But abuse survivors go overboard. They survive on their dreams rather than trusting that the reality would be better than the fantasy. Reality may be too depressing, frightening, and unsure for them to allow themselves to experience it.

Where It Comes From

Discomfort with the thought of being in a real love relationship is usually the genesis of fantasy relationships. Avoiding real commitment or being seen for who you are, searching for a person who is good for you, and even defining what you really want can be overwhelming and maybe not even possible until you see how the abuse has separated you from who you really are.

Still, a fantasy life can be a nice way to define what you *hope* for in a real partner someday. Just be aware that the person you use to fantasize may be so weak and mild that they only appear to be who you think they are. Ultimately, the real person will emerge and you might be disappointed in them for not living up to your expectations. You may feel angry and betrayed, or even embarrassed because your lover can't live up to your needs. The acting exercises can help you get deeper insights into what your fantasy life is telling you about what you really want in a relationship.

Creating Your Own Personality with Fantasy

Another facet of fantasy is the desire to change who you are entirely by creating your own personality, usually one that you believe will be more acceptable to others. Abuse survivors feel a need to make up a strong, definite personality, someone they imagine other people would like them to be. That is one way they try to fit in.

These fantasies can become very involved as survivors mentally figure out what kind of music they should listen to, what kind of books their "perfect" persona would read, the kind of art they'd like or what theater they would go to, what dates they'd pick, and what kind of "look" (clothes, makeup, etc.) they'd have. This might even extend to the professions they feel they should follow to help them feel they are being what others want them to be.

Sometimes survivors live their entire lives in their heads, creating experiences that they believe make them more valuable, more lovable, and certainly more exciting to others. It's always easier to create the fantasy than to work toward the reality, especially when you have not found out how to believe in yourself, and you don't trust how things could really turn out.

Many clients have described a desire to change their names as a way of escaping their pasts. One client, Elizabeth, went to great extremes to try on "new names" by pairing two street signs together!

Where It Comes From

Abuse survivors often feel they can't afford to reveal their true selves for fear others will find out about the abuse or suspect what has happened to them. They want to start over completely. Changing your identity by picking a new name or new persona is a way of trying to be someone else entirely—someone who was never abused. It's a way of beginning again with a totally different history where no abuse took place.

Our minds and bodies *want* to be connected, so we can get into a lot of trouble trying to keep them apart. So use your rich fantasy life to find a real love. Make fantasies work for you in your real world. That way you will live a life of having rather than just wishing.

Sexualizing Relationships Where No Sex Exists

You have undoubtedly known people who think everyone is coming on to him or her sexually. The simplest, most innocuous "hello" can be construed as a sexual moment. Many abuse survivors cannot recognize which relationships are friendships and which are possible intimate partnerships. Sexualizing every relationship comes out of needing romance, while being afraid of having it. Or it comes out of a need for caring and understanding from a lover. A client of mine was losing her mother to cancer. As she visited her mother on the hospital ward one afternoon, a doctor who was one of the team caring for her ailing parent was kind to her and asked my client if she needed a ride home. This simple act of caring caused my client to get a crush on the doctor as a way of not concentrating on her mother's horrible illness. It had the effect of enabling my client to continue going to the ward to see her mother, day after day, remain optimistic in front of her, and deal with all the ramifications of helping a terminally ill patient cope.

Some abuse survivors, especially sexual-abuse survivors, believe that the only asset they have to give anyone is their sexuality. These survivors might act in a sexy manner, dress suggestively, or are, in fact, promiscuous. The fantasy of appearing sexy is more exciting than the reality of being sexy. By using acting exercises and therapy, people who believe their only worth is sexuality can begin to explore other ways of dealing in the world. That can be a freeing and exciting experience because it allows you different ways of offering your worth to others.

Where It Comes From

Sexualizing every relationship comes out of the need to avoid real sexual experience. It is a way to stay in the safety of fantasy. And fantasy, as you know by now, means total control over the outcome—at least in your mind. In fantasy you can create the illusion of a satisfying sexual relationship, even if you feel you can't have one in reality. Isolation and fantasy are two ways of never having to feel betrayed, frightened, or abandoned. Sexual fantasy appears to offer immediate excitement in the confines of safety.

Abuse survivors also fantasize that a relationship they are in will meet all their needs. But dreaming that you are already successful in some endeavor, one you may never have even tried, or dreaming of the "day it will happen" is also a way of feeling the success you need without having to go through the trials and tribulations of getting there, without having to risk losing anything for that success.

But don't fret about having thoughts of fantasy sex. Remember, fantasy sex is an excellent way to begin defining what you eventually really want. The exercises are tailor-made to help you channel your wants and wishes into reality.

Crushes and Other Power Reducers

Everyone has normal, garden-variety crushes. They're normal. The problems come when you blindly believe they are real. Crushes can serve a myriad of needs for abuse survivors. Having a crush on someone inappropriate, cruel, or actively hostile is another way a survivor can put him or herself in the inferior position in a relationship. The same position they probably felt as a child and one that feels "right" or familiar to them. Crushes can reduce your respect for yourself because you give all your power away to the other person. It is a repetition compulsion: The abuser had all the power over you in the past and you may have defined that as love. So, now you feel powerless again. That may be exactly how you see love now in an adult relationship. That's why you give your power away—in the guise of a crush. When you have a crush on someone, you don't see the real person— you see what you want to see. You might even see yourself feeding someone else's ego in the hopes they will love you all the more for making them feel strong and good. Most crushes are not reciprocated, so you end up feeling betrayed.

If you are the type who spends most of your time worrying about how your love interest perceives you, you will run out of ways to keep him or her. Remember, fears of abandonment fuel our desire to please our partner. Survivors who inadvertently choose judgmental people as partners will do anything the partner wants in order not to lose them, so instead they end up losing sight of who *they* are and what *they* want.

Although you might feel temporary relief in fantasy, you will still know your relationship is not true, open, or giving. That will fuel your insecurity, so you become afraid that the minute someone else with more money or a better situation comes along, you will be dumped. The guarantees you want are not really there, so you need to be able to trust your ability to sustain a relationship first.

Where It Comes From

The need to have love on your own terms is probably the genesis of crushes. The need to control love and the need to create a wonderful, conflict-free, totally romantic relationship fuels the crush. We all want to believe the perfect person is out there for us: someone who is totally devoted, understanding, and loving but who is also exciting and knows and can deal with our every mood. Movies and television offer "soap opera" types of love affairs, and they can look so enticing. But the right chemistry and understanding with a real person can create the most exciting relationship of all.

Lying and the Desire to Be Seen Differently

Lying, like changing your name or affecting a new identity, is just another ploy to become someone more desirable—or rather, someone who you believe would be more desirable. Lying offers a respite from feeling left out, abandoned, and isolated. It gives the illusion of being okay.

Where It Comes From

As you probably have already suspected, lying is a defense to help you feel strong, give you the kind of identity you think others would accept, and to artificially enhance your self-esteem.

Heather used to lie about everything, even when it wasn't necessary. She had attended a wonderful university but insisted that she had gone to Harvard. She would repeat stories she heard from others and pretend they were hers. She became the star of every lie. Her lies were easily uncovered by others, but that did not deter her. As she uncovered who she really was with acting exercises, she also found that her need to lie diminished. She began to accept herself and actually liked who she was.

Talking Against Your Lover in an Otherwise Good Relationship

I remember a girl who was engaged to be married talking disgracefully about her fiancée. She wanted to know if others saw him as revolting as she did: not good-looking, no big prize. At first I was appalled at the way she described him—even making fun of his sexuality at a party. I couldn't figure out why she would even consider marrying someone she respected so little.

This might seem an odd place to put in a discussion of talking against your lover. But fantasy plays a role here, too. Survivors can feel so insecure about their ability to maintain a relationship that they try to minimize its importance by talking against their partner to their friends or colleagues. The survivor may actually be very much in love, but this feeling is the very reason for trying to make the relationship appear less, so that if it does end, the survivor won't feel abandoned and alone.

Where It Comes From

This problem may be an extension of your own feelings of revulsion about yourself: Why would anyone want me? The old Groucho Marx joke fits again: "I wouldn't want to belong to any club that accepted me as a member." But, besides the fear that you are not worthy of anyone wonderful, there might also be a real panic that you could lose a terrific partner. This might be the only one who will ever be interested in you, and you could lose him or her. Fear of loss is often a reason to minimize what you have. It doesn't work, because it's too late already: you are in love, and you want this relationship to last, but you are afraid it won't. Deep down, you're probably afraid that this love will be destroyed the same way your unconditional parental love was shattered by abuse.

Manipulating the Relationship with Money or Power

Some survivors hope to begin to trust by trusting only in the concrete, tangible aspects of a relationship such as financial support, someone helping their career, or a partner being accommodating or anticipating and providing for their needs most of the time. Money and power are concrete. We allow others to be selfish and uncaring toward us—just as long as they don't leave us and keep on helping and providing for us.

Many abuse survivors feel the only proof of someone's love for them comes in how much that person can give them. On the other hand, some survivors feel that buying a partner guarantees loyalty and devotion. Both are ways of depending on outside elements to ensure true love. Only inner trust and the ability to recognize who is right for you and who is wrong will guarantee your best chance at a good relationship.

Where It Comes From

As I said, money and power are concrete, and they also represent power and control, something survivors are always seeking. We want *proof* that something we do will be the decisive factor in whether or not someone loves us. But that proof is illusory. The only way we can know if someone cares is to see what they do and how they act toward us. Some survivors seek executive positions where the power differential includes underlings who need the survivor to help them gain or keep work. Others look for out-of-work partner who must depend on the survivor for food and shelter.

In adulthood, abuse survivors often try to be *like the abuser*—they want to have the same power over others that the abuser had over them. Survivors who manipulate relationships with money and power are trying to turn the tables around to see what it's like to have the power by putting themselves in the place of the abuser. They may simply want to know what that kind of power feels like, or they may want to find out what was exciting about the abuse for the abuser. One of the quickest ways to feel strong is to wield power over a partner.

Child abuse is defined by domination. Using money and power seems to offer you control, and control is what most abuse survivors crave. So often the abuser was the "star of the show" in their house. You had no ability to outshine him or her. You had no power or control. Manipulation offers both, and in a way that can make you look exciting. You may feel that no one can hurt you if you are the one holding the strings. But too soon you will probably feel manipulated and used yourself. So it's important to overcome the need to control others and begin to learn how to nurture and be nurtured equally.

There are other, more hidden aspects to using money and power for control: they can be a way the survivor "models" for another person what he or she wants. Buying a relationship can also help us feel guarded against being judged, a fear many survivors seem to carry around. Even opinions of others can be bought, if the survivor believes the partner "owes" him or her something. And judgment by someone "beneath" you has a less devastating impact than being judged by someone "over" you in power.

Sleeping with Many Partners When You Are in a Monogamous Relationship

Sexual addiction, or sleeping with many people when you are supposedly in a monogamous relationship, is one way survivors hide their intimacy problems and feel in control. Indiscriminate sexual involvement can feel like proof that you're powerful, sexy, and "worth it" because you are able to gain attention and physical love from so many people.

The excitement of giving yourself and someone else immediate pleasure can be very addictive, especially if you are in a boring job or career and need outside thrills to balance out your life. Unfortunately, too often there is a sense of emptiness afterward because these lovers mean nothing in the long run.

Where It Comes From

As in most addictive behavior, sexual addiction is mainly about escape from intimacy and fear of loss. But the obvious problem of involving yourself with multiple lovers is that you are denying yourself true, meaningful relationships. Indiscriminate sexual behavior may also unconsciously reflect your preference to remain alone in order to feel independent. At least then, you think, you can't be hurt again. But hiding behind many relationships and preventing yourself from settling with one good partner can ultimately increase loneliness.

Prematurely Leaving the Relationship (or, Splitting Revisited)

Do you feel people let you down? First they seem "good," then they seem "bad," then they seem "good" again. We often can't decide how to treat a loved one. Survivors sometimes employ the splitting dynamic of "good" or "bad."

Haven't we all known people who say, "Well, he didn't put the top on the toothpaste, that's it, he's out of here." Survivors may also not be able to discriminate between what is simply a spat and what is an ending. You, too, might feel that having someone too close is just too much, so you distance yourself for protection by using any means possible to get rid of the intruder. But prematurely leaving a good relationship is just another power play.

It takes insight to begin to see the whole picture so that you can relate to real issues before you throw your partner out. And insight comes from employing exercises that trick your unconscious into expressing itself verbally and freely, rather than with "acting out" behavior. As you talk to your inner self through the exercises, you will discover many ways to make an unfortunate situation right without having to abruptly leave it in order to feel independent and powerful.

Where It Comes From

Even in therapy, resistant clients may feel the need to leave the therapeutic relationship before (they think) the therapist leaves them. Survivors would rather end a relationship before the relationship dies or ends up out of their control. Many times you hear of people sabotaging a good thing in their lives for fear that it will turn out badly anyway. At least if they do something to mess it up, there will be a reason for the disappointment and they will have had some control over the outcome, too.

You have probably experienced telephone conversations where you feel the need to get off the phone before the other person hangs up. It may feel like you are in control and your dignity is intact if you make a point of hanging up first. Our old sense of mistrust in the world rears its ugly head when we are getting in "too deeply" in a relationship or any hopeful situation.

Alcohol, Drugs, and Other Addictions

Intrusive memories of trauma and abuse usually come up unexpectedly during passion or other emotional times when your greatest hope is to concentrate on what is going on in the moment—like lovemaking, for instance. Drinking, using drugs, or other addictions can be the only way survivors might initially feel they're in charge of their feelings.

Drugs and alcohol might stop these thoughts temporarily, but there are always memories that don't seem to go away. As long as these memories have no "cure," no lessening, we revert back to them, so alcohol or drugs may seem welcome panaceas and briefly seem to tame these unwanted thoughts. It's almost as if we cannot allow ourselves to have true joy until these memories are dealt with and overcome.

Where It Comes From

Alcohol can initially help you create a false sense of confidence and self-assuredness that soon dissipates as you become used to the substance and need more and more of it to create the same feelings. Unfortunately, alcohol and drug intake is often used as a way of "numbing out" or escaping during sex. But remember, although substance use numbs what is happening at the moment, as the drug wears off, this numbing can give way to more fear, heightened mistrust, and anger at partners. All this anxiety can actually create an inability to have an orgasm altogether. Sooner or later, you want to enjoy your lover and lovemaking without needing outside help.

An alcoholic prefers to "stiffen" him or herself up to whatever is happening. They might think they can control the emotions and feelings surrounding the relationship better if they are drinking and using drugs. Or they might tell themselves they can do anything as long as they're drunk. Many actors have told me in therapy that they needed alcohol to muster up tears in a scene, or they used substances because they felt they helped the actors be more real, more raw in a scene. If they are playing an alcoholic who is currently drunk, perhaps they will achieve some of that reality, but it will be they who are drunk, not the character—and it's the character we want to see drunk!

In real life, too, substance abuse makes you or the substance abuser you are involved with not present—not there for you. Even in sex, alcohol numbs after it initially excites, and after a while it stops working altogether.

In the next chapter, you will work on communication exercises to deal with interactions with real, live people. That will undoubtedly prove to be a much more satisfying experience in the long run.

I remember a well-known actress who showed up for auditions drunk. She felt she was more "real" when she was loaded. After years of working this way, she finally landed a reading for an important television series. She got extra drunk for this audition. When she'd finished, the casting room smelled of booze, the casting director had to help her out into the hallway, and there the director told her he would never use her again. In the parking lot, the actress got into her car, picked up the open bottle of vodka that had normally been her "friend," and threw it out the car window so that it smashed on the concrete of the studio lot. The booze had let her down. She went home, went to bed, and when she awoke, she called an Alcoholics Anonymous group and began her recovery. In therapy, she used all the exercises to gently help herself discover and overcome her need to feel safe by numbing herself so that she could become immune to judgment and criticism.

Bullying

Withholding feelings, the silent treatment, not speaking to someone about what is bothering you, and threatening your partner with violence, or with no sex are all ways of bullying. Sometimes embarrassing someone by yelling at them in public or forcing a "scene" are ways of gaining control and bullying your partner into doing what you want. For the person doing the bullying, it might feel empowering, and that person will probably feel in control for the moment. But retaliation is usually what happens when your partner feels bullied.

No one wants to feel vulnerable, so he or she will find ways of making *you* scared and insecure. It becomes another vicious circle.

Where It Comes From

As you probably have already guessed, bullying comes from having been bullied. We want to feel the power and control our abusers felt, so we act the way they did. There are many ways we recreate for ourselves what the abuser did to us. Sometimes we unwittingly recreate the same situation. When I hear that a child has hit another child at school, my first question to the aggressor is, "Who is hitting you?" You would be surprised at the answers. A child does what he or she sees, and later in adulthood, the memories of what was done to you linger until you work them through. Until then, there is always an eager desire to discover what the excitement was for the abuser.

If you find bullying is your relationship issue, perhaps conflict and confrontation are at the root of your acting out. You don't want to fight with anyone. But healthy fighting can be healing and powerful, helping you realize you don't need to split your feelings between all good and all bad. Use the exercises to express your anger, resentment, concern, or fears in a healthy way, and find other ways of having your partner hear you. That is intimacy.

Using the Relationship to Recreate the Abuse Situation

Whether or not they want to or whether or not they deliberately try not to, survivors who have not recovered from abuse will almost surely recreate with their current lover the exact abuse situation they had with their abuser. Many survivors find abusive, punishing relationships by looking for others who will abuse them in a way similar to how they were abused in their childhood. But in the end, repetition compulsion will feel like an old picture we've seen many, many times that we can notice but not be particularly affected by anymore.

Relationships may appear exciting and different from previous ones, but as they go on, it becomes apparent that the same familiar patterns are emerging. When you recognize how you are drawn into these types of relationships, you can begin to stop complying with abusers. Even the smallest change in behavior will enable a more desirable relationship to come your way.

My friend Anita only enjoyed abusive, cruel men who made her feel they would leave her. In the same way her mother abandoned her when she was a baby becasue her mother's boyfriend didn't want children. Whenever a kind, devoted lover presented himself, she would shun him as boring and uninteresting. She left a well-educated and kind person who cared for her for a man who stayed out most of the night, and who was abusive and demeaning in bed.

But, if you think about it, the original situation in which you discovered sex and love probably was fraught with fear, pain, shame, and embarrassment. Your challenge now is how to separate the abuser from your current lover. How can you make love to a current partner without substituting or recreating the abuse situation and ruining your pleasure? One way is to discover other ways of exciting yourself besides the original abuse situation. With acting exercises, you can begin to tease apart and divide abusive yet exciting actions from nonabusive but equally exciting actions.

Where It Comes From

Finding another abusive relationship may feel like an accident. But remember, the unconscious mind is searching for peace, and one of the ways it may find it is to hide feelings of personal isolation, stigma, and humiliation in a relationship that affords a focal point on which these feelings can be blamed. One that is familiar. Abuse survivors may have never experienced any other kind of relationship than a battering one, a sexually abusive one, or an emotionally cruel one. Anger becomes the only emotion they can trust.

Now let's take a look at some communication exercises that partners can do together.

Chapter 26

Acting Exercises for Couples

Origins of Dysfunctional Behavior in Relationships

It is hard to remain in a relationship in which you feel the other person is really secretly using you, or needs something from you, but doesn't really love you. That is probably how you felt when you were being abused. So, understandably, the most common aftereffects of past abuse that crop up in relationships encompass blaming, lowered expectations, or disappointments with partners. The disappointment in not getting your needs met sexually, financially, or emotionally leads to anger and further degradation in your relationship and in other parts of your life.

How Exercises Bring Up Real Emotions

You probably will find that having completed the exercises and techniques described in this book has brought back many memories of how you conduct yourself in relationships. The exercises are used to help bring up real feelings that have been glossed over by fantasy, wishful thinking, and escape tactics. Almost all therapies are there to help you look at the reality of your situation rather than fantasy or what you *wish* were the truth so that you can change what you don't want and keep what is good for you. Undoubtedly, you will discover that once the truth has surfaced, bad or dissatisfying relationships will be phased out of your life. What will appear in their place will be good relationships with people who respect and value you for who you are.

Communication Exercises

The most effective exercises for abuse survivors in relationships are the communication exercises. They offer a chance for survivors to communicate in an improvisational form. You will notice that you will really connect to another person and hear their responses.

Creating a Balance

These exercises are designed to help survivors unblock developmental obstacles that have caused them to be afraid of abandonment on the one hand and enmeshment on the other.

When doing the communication exercises, you may find that relationship questions come up, such as: "Do I always need to be at one end of the nurturing spectrum or the other?" "Can I find a place in the middle where I can avoid both extremes—the terror of being left alone or the fear of being smothered?" Perhaps you can find a comfortable place within the exercises where you will discover that you can play both parts—nurturer and nurtured.

Eye to Eye Exercise

This exercise helps you and your partner keep your whole focus on each other. No words are ever spoken. Simply notice the feelings that come up as you gaze into each other's eyes: shyness, coyness, embarrassment, shame, fear, love, or any combination.

1. Sit facing each other. No touching or physical contact.
2. Stare into each other's eyes without averting your gaze.
3. The minute someone looks away, the exercise is over.
4. Keep gazing into the other person's eyes. Notice what feelings come up for you. Usually people will start laughing, but emotions soon turn more serious. You may find yourself crying, angry, confused, or worried.
5. Just allow the emotions to come up and identify them out loud, if you wish.
6. Stop the exercise when you feel you have received and given as much nonverbal communication as you were able, or until the other person averts his or her gaze.
7. Now face forward without looking at each other.
8. Take turns describing the kinds of emotions that came up.
9. Turn and face each other again.

10. Take turns describing to the other person what you want, need, and what you got out of the exercise.

The Mutual Connection Exercise

This is a verbal exercise. It is improvisational in that one of the partners will have three minutes to search for something the other partner has hidden. Have your partner leave the room temporarily until you hide an important, personal object. When you feel the object has been well hidden, sit in a chair in the middle of the room. Then you can alert your partner to come back into the room.

The objective of this exercise is that the person who has left the room will look for the hidden object once he or she comes back into the room. Once they find the hidden object, or their time is up, the exercise is over.

1. Begin the exercise by having no expectations of what or how you will communicate with your partner.
2. Have your partner leave the room.
3. Find one personal object from the past and hide that somewhere in the room.
4. Now sit in the middle of the room.
5. Call your partner back.
6. It is your job to steer your partner closer to the object without telling them where it is. You can say, "You're close, " or, "No, you are nowhere near it." The questions can't be a variation on "Where is the object?" obviously. Your partner will ask "close" or "few" questions only. The partner will say either "Yes, you are close" or "No, you are not close." This keeps the searching partner on his or her toes, always scanning the other partner's face and mannerisms to see what clues might be gotten from those actions.
7. As you speak to your partner, you can request, warn, or demand, and your partner will either realize he or she is close to the spot where the object is hidden or is far away.
8. Once your partner has either uncovered the object, or time is up, the exercise is over.

Richard and Louise's Story

Richard and Louise had lived together for five years, but when Richard blamed, Louise became defensive and angry. Louise enjoyed doing this exercise because it allowed Richard to see how he blamed her, even though he adamantly denied doing so. Louise hid a charm he had given her. When he came out from behind the screen in my office, he looked in the usual places, behind a chair, in a desk drawer. But Louise had hidden the charm where it was supposed to be—around her neck. Her high collar kept it from view.

As Richard came closer and closer to Louise, she gave signs by smiling, even saying "You're close," until Richard finally found the charm. It never occurred to him to look in the most obvious of places, and her hints made it possible for him to concentrate solely on their communication together.

Remember: Something must always trigger your dialogue. Don't speak just to be speaking.

The Trust Exercise

This exercise is a favorite of acting classes and is even used in the military! That's how good it is at helping you begin to trust another person.

1. Put a large mattress or other heavy, soft material on the floor. You will be using this as a safety net in case you fall backward, so make sure it is soft, strong, and can withstand your fall.

2. Both you and your partner stand on the mattress, one in front of the other, one facing the other's back.

3. The person whose back is to their partner will now allow themselves to fall backward into the partner's arms.

4. The partner will put out his or her arms to catch the fall before the first person falls onto the mattress.

5. Trust comes because you are trusting that your partner will catch you before you fall backward onto the mattress.

6. Each partner trusts the other to do this exercise.

7. Discuss feelings together when you both have had a chance to experience the other person catching you.

The "Put Your Partner on a Pedestal" Exercise

Too many abuse survivors need to find that loving parent. They find instead a partner who can substitute for their parent by being smarter, better looking, in a more powerful job or profession, or in some other situation that makes the survivor feel the partner is above them and better than they are. In life, it is important to have feelings of your *own* worth. This next exercise will allow you to develop an understanding of what you want and admire in a partner, and how you can own these same qualities in yourself. If you are looking for a doctor, why aren't *you* a doctor? If you are looking for a "moneymaker," why aren't *you* a moneymaker? Get the point? We are looking for people who we want to admire—so admire yourself first.

1. Ask your partner to sit in a chair.
2. You sit on the floor next to the chair.
3. Look at your partner.
4. Describe to your partner how you feel sitting on the floor next to them.
5. Describe how you think the partner might be feeling in the chair.
6. Now begin a conversation with your partner: you on the floor, the partner in the chair.
7. As the conversation continues, each of you get up and *slowly* begin to change places so that you end up in the chair, and your partner ends up sitting on the floor.
8. As you change places, continue your conversation and interject when you feel it is appropriate about how you are feeling inside with this movement.
9. When each of you has changed places, discuss how you feel: you in the chair, and your partner now on the floor.
10. Discuss what emotions and feelings came up for you.

In the next chapter we will see how each person is unique, and yet recovery is not so different for each one of us.

Chapter 27

What Determines Recovery?

What Determines Recovery: What Have I Achieved?

Support, caring friends and family and self-investigation all aid in recovery from child abuse. But, after you know where it all comes from, what then? Well, hopefully you will have uncovered many memories, old patterns, and survival tactics that you have used to feel safe and secure, but which haven't always worked the way you had hoped. Now you have achieved a way of discovering who you are, what you want, and how you can go about getting it. Perhaps you also discovered certain negative directions you took that you now realize you can avoid in the future.

Recovering abuse survivors are very different from those who have not recovered. Recoverers usually have more self-esteem, are more aware of what they want, trust themselves more with others, and are able to feel secure inside rather than search for their security outside. Mostly, they have no more secrets and they are proud of having overcome shame. It's important for you to look at the difference so that you can decide how to best steer your recovery, and so that you can realize your success in feeling good and living a happy life. People who have been abused have much in common with others who have suffered the same fate. Still, severity, frequency, and force of abuse are deciding factors in how well or poorly a person will *recover* from their abuse. Almost all agree that focused, involved perseverance in discovering who you are will best help you to recover fast.

Confusion about what you are supposed to feel can also play a part in your recovery. Your family or friends may urge you in direct or subtle ways to "just get over it," but I always ask those people, "How? Don't you think if they could, they would?" One client, Barbara, described an unfeeling therapist who told her, "Forget about it. So what if you were sexually abused as a child? We're sexual people." The guilt and confusion stemming from that kind of response—especially from those who are supposed to listen and validate you—can be a real impediment to recovery.

An abuse survivor might try to tell herself or himself that she must be "sick" to blame her abuser—that her abuser really didn't mean anything by it: "They didn't mean to be inappropriate; they were just being loving." Attributing blame to those who actually hurt you, without taking it out on yourself, is healing.

Go to a school and watch the kids playing. Go to a park and see children who are now the age you were when you were abused. Would you seriously blame them? Or are you much more likely to blame the perpetrator? As I have said so many times in this book, it is easy for survivors to end up blaming themselves for thinking they created the scenario of an abuse. They may even begin doubting that the abuse really happened. And if the survivor has no support for their story, they begin to feel even more damaged, reclusive, and dirty. That's when they want to punish themselves by self-mutilation, sabotage, and creating problems. The truth is, if you feel you were abused, you were! It is the aftermath of the abuse that determines how catastrophic it was for you.

Don't compare your abuse with anyone else's. Each person's abuse is different, and each person's perspective on their abuse will be unique. The trick is to be able to look at what happened to you, how it happened, how it affects you now, and then integrate the anger, hurt, and sadness so that you can finally control it and live your life in freedom.

Another strong determinant of how long it takes you to recover is your perception of the abuse. Feeling you contributed to it, or made it dirty when it was seemingly innocent, can cause you to maintain devastating feelings of shame and humiliation. At least intellectually remember this: The abuser is *always* to blame. Survivors have a hard time believing this.

One Person's Recovery: Lou's Story

Lou was a thirty-five-year-old thief. She had started out life as a sweet little girl who came from the Philippines with her family. Once in the U.S., her father lost his job, divorced her mother, and Lou was left with a divided family. Her three sisters were sent back to Manila and she was left alone with a very depressed mother.

Her mother remarried when Lou was sixteen, and her stepfather began a long series of sexual assaults on her. At first Lou threatened to tell her mother. But when she did, Lou's mom called her a liar and wouldn't believe anything she said. At seventeen, Lou became pregnant with her stepfather's child, and still her mother denied what was happening in their household.

When Lou got an abortion, her stepfather beat her so badly that she ended up in the hospital. That's where I met her. Her face was so ravaged by punching and slapping that at first it was almost impossible to see her features. She was too numbed and dispirited to even cry as she told me what happened that day.

Her stepfather began to attack her sexually. He pushed her into her room, onto her bed, and began to tear off her clothes. As they began to have sex, she told him that she had aborted the child. He became outraged, furious, and out of control. He began punching her while they were in the middle of having sex. He broke her nose, ripped her ear, and pulled large amounts of hair out of her head.

A neighbor heard Lou screaming and called the police. Upon hearing the sirens, Lou's stepfather jumped off her and grabbed a shotgun. Luckily, it was empty, and when the police forced their way into the house, he was easily arrested and handcuffed. Lou was taken to the hospital.

Lou told me that nothing in her life had ever felt real. She always felt she was different from others, isolated and alone. In therapy, Lou began to use the exercises, starting with the Coffee Cup Exercise where she created a miniature scene from Christmas the year her mother and father began fighting. She described her childhood as completely unpredictable. On days where happiness and pleasure should preside, like Christmas or someone's birthday, you could bet that unhappiness and tension existed instead.

She began to recreate her entire life, beginning in the Philippines. It was three weeks before she could even begin to get into her emotional life to the point where I began to think the exercises might not be the right way for her to deal with memories and feelings. But together—slowly and gently—we pressed on. One day, during the Sunshine Exercise, she remembered the heat of the islands and the secret, nonverbal ways of her family. Nothing was ever spoken about or acknowledged. She felt she was constantly living in a dream where the next action in her life would be unknown, a mystery. Distorted and unconnected events seemed the norm in her family of origin. The Portrait Exercise reminded her of the person she wished she could have been before the abuse started. She found out during the Animal Exercise that she had felt like a tiny ferret, alone and at the mercy of anyone around. The Fourth Wall Exercise found her creating a room with a wall covered in tokens, statues, and honors for her work—she just wasn't sure what kind of work that would be. In her Private Moment Exercise, she was the angel on the top of the Christmas tree, which is just how she wanted to feel. During the Telephone Exercise she found herself talking to her real father. She wanted to love him and tell him that.

She used the Atmosphere Exercise, which proved to be a turning point in helping her recreate her childhood. She recreated the smell of mustiness and putrid, old alcohol that permeated her home. As she sat back in the chair in my office she began to remember the raw feelings she had in her closed-off room at home.

Using the "As If" Exercise, Lou made herself feel as if she were a giant who could crush anyone who tried to hurt her. It was amazing to see how she was gentle and simply made the intruder go away without wanting to crush him or hurt him back.

Finally, as she began the internal exercises, she found that the Dying Exercise caused her the most trouble. She wanted to go back and change everything that had happened, but she knew she couldn't. So instead, she decided to try to live from this moment on. She described how things could be different, where she needed to be physically and mentally so that her life could change and she could become truly successful. The Sense Memory Exercise helped her create objects she wanted to give to other people—tokens of love and appreciation. She found a healing and a spirituality that would have been difficult for many.

Lou did a Building a Room Exercise and combined it with the Preparation-Before-a-Scene Exercise so that she could create a time when she would gather her whole family together and tell them what had happened to her, how she had dealt with her problems, and now, how she was healing herself. During the Affective Memory Exercise, which needed to be a dramatic incident at least seven years old, she created her first sexual abuse encounter. In it, she was able to describe all her feelings and was able to deal with the anger and hatred she had harbored for her abuser. But she was always too scared to confront him.

As she was able to gain attention and respect from me, her newfound strength and her self-esteem grew and enabled her to work through problems and needs in her life in a way she never realized was possible.

As she continued the hierarchy of exercises, more and more memories surfaced. She seemed to be able to tolerate them confidently and safely. No real fear was involved, and I realized she was monitoring her own ability to deal with what had happened in her life, and she was doing it very well. The acting exercises were giving her the control she had always lacked. In fact, how far she went with the exercises was her first real control over what was happening in her life. She could do as little or as much as she needed to with each exercise.

Each time she attempted the Affective Memory Exercise, more memories surfaced and she was able to contain and deal with each one in a way she had never known was possible.

To temper these recollections, Lou made good use of her "third eye" exercise, which is that part of you that keeps you aware at all times of where you really are and what you are really doing. It also allows you to stop any exercise before you feel overwhelmed by it.

As Lou remembered her stepfather's visits to her room, the noises and voices surrounding his visits became vividly apparent. These recreated sights and sounds triggered feelings about the images of her room at home so that she could reexperience them now as an adult and congeal the fragmentation she had always felt. She remembered how hard she had tried to appease everyone while "being scared to death." She also remembered that she needed to guess what everyone was thinking in order to feel safe.

As the memories continued to flow, we began to do exercises to help her slow down the process even further—at times she was going much too fast and ran the risk of leaving my office overwhelmed with fear and anxiety. When I told her that I thought some of her deeper work should go more slowly, she told me that she wanted to "cure" herself immediately. The acting exercises I offered her at this point (as all the exercises in this book) allowed her to control how fast and